# ARIZONA UNDER THE SUN

# ARIZONA
# Under the Sun

by

## Oren Arnold

With a Foreword by Barry Goldwater

The Bond Wheelwright Company, Freeport, Maine

*The author is deeply grateful to the more than*
*one hundred librarians, teachers, editors and other*
*authorities on Arizona lore who helped in preparation*
*and checking of the manuscript for this book.*

*First Edition*

*Manufactured in the United States of America*
*in Canada:   Abelard-Schuman Ltd., 869 Queen Street West, Toronto 3*

Dedicated to

G. BARTER BELL

*Good Arizonan*
*Good Neighbor*
*Good Friend*

# PREFACE

For no real reason, many persons cling to the feeling that any book about a state is inescapably an attempt at history. This fallacy must not prejudice the reader here. Pure history is fine — in its place. But it is also very likely to become too analytical, too detailed, too tedious for enjoyment and assimilation, which is why relatively few people bother to read it.

ARIZONA UNDER THE SUN is not history, it is a portrait.

It is presented on a broad and splashy canvas, partly realistic, partly impressionistic, but totally personal. To be sure, *some* history is included; anything that happened even yesterday is history, in a sense. But the over-all picture is not one of chronological yester-year, it is Arizona as I have seen and loved it, Arizona as it is today. The stated facts have been carefully checked for accuracy (though a few are controversial). There is no exaggeration for emphasis — none was necessary; a simple statement of things as they are here is exciting enough. There is no straining for scholarliness or "literary style" or any such pompous nonsense, because that would be quite out of harmony with the state's ruggedly wonderful informality.

Let the academicians remain in Boston; let the happy people come ride our wild free hills.

O. A.

*Phoenix*

ix

# CONTENTS

xi

# FOREWORD

Even getting up at 3 o'clock in the morning, I faced a tight schedule. I had to clean a pile of correspondence off my desk, fly to San Francisco for the wedding of my younger son Mike, and then take off with my wife Peggy on a trip to South Africa and Rhodesia. Somewhere in the pile were the proof sheets of Oren Arnold's *Arizona Under the Sun*. I would pack them and find time for reading in transit. First, I'd just take a look. That was my mistake.

When I came to, a couple of hours later, my itinerary was a mess and I didn't mind. Pick up anything that Oren writes, and you're captured. That's especially true when he writes about something he knows so well and loves as much as he does Arizona. Thank heavens, Oren isn't jealous. He's willing to share his love with the world.

I've spent a lifetime in the Territory and State of Arizona. It was a small place, and now it's a big place. It has led the nation in practically every growth index that matters. And I know why. The answer is people.

We are indebted to the Anasazi, who lived here as long as 15,000 years ago, for much of our culture. We are indebted to the Indians who have lived here some 2,500 years; and we still live with their culture, language, music and art. And we are indebted to the early Spaniards and the later Mexicans. Moreover, we modern Arizonans are indebted to every State in the Union and many foreign countries for the people who have come here in the past hundred years. Oren is one of them. It speaks volumes for the magnetism of the Sunshine State to note that Oren started with a deep affection for his native Texas, and transferred it to Arizona. And people keep on coming here from everywhere, for the warmth of our sun and the warmth of our friendship.

A newspaper in the southern part of the State asked me to make a forecast concerning the year 2012, when Arizona will observe its statehood centennial. My arithmetic has never been too good, but I think I was just about right in predicting a population of 18 million, with Phoenix one of the five or six biggest cities in the United States. All those growth indicators keep going in the same direction.

Sometimes the trouble with us natives is that we take the place too much for granted. If you want to find out whether a resident is a native, just ask him a question about the State's history or one of its natural wonders; if he can answer, chances are ten to one he's from out of state. If he can answer just about every question anybody can ask about Arizona, chances are he's Oren Arnold. We hope he's around a long, long time, to supply our grandchildren and great-grandchildren with the kind of enjoyable reading he has provided us.

I have sometimes laughingly labeled Oren the "manana" man. He won't do it today if he can put if off until tomorrow, I said; and he won't do it tomorrow, either, unless it benefits somebody. Well, I'm grateful he hasn't waited till some distant tomorrow to write this book, because it can benefit so many of us today.

Millions of Americans who have never had any special interest in Arizona will find themselves just a little prouder of this whole land of ours. They'll be reading, with a can't-put-it-down interest, about 114,000 square miles of America which offers unrivaled natural wonders, warmth of sun and beauty of sky, charm of people and love of life. Everybody who knows Arizona feels it; only a gifted few can express it. Oren Arnold does both — and, I think, better than anybody.

BARRY GOLDWATER

*December 4, 1967*

# I. SUN AND SKY AND ROOM-ENOUGH

## 1. West, O West

If you have been reared in sun-bathed Arizona, you inevitably take many wonderful things for granted. But if you are a newcomer from some distant area you experience many exciting adventures and surprises. Happily, however, the newcomer nearly always helps the native re-discover his homeland; points him toward a fresh and exhilarating experience. This has nothing to do with ballyhoo or "boosting" or chamber of commercialism; rather is it a dawning cultural or esthetic sensitivity, an awareness of nuances subtler than cold carlot shipments and bank accounts.

Let's say that you are a prototype, a new arrival from New York City. Your first reaction when you get out of your train, car, or plane and begin to look around is likely to be an exclamation — "It's so BIG out here!"

And you'll be right. The West *is* big; bigger, roomier, than even the westerner suspects. You may have spent many a happy afternoon strolling in your city's beautiful Central Park, a fine wooded area with lakes and trails, and considered it truly a big open area. Truth is, all of Manhattan Island has fewer than

1

25,000 acres. In Arizona one man alone *stole* 12,000,000 acres! (See Chapter 6) Our newspapers often announce the sale of ranches exceeding 100,000 acres.

Back east, the traveler is almost never out of sight of a city, town, home, store or filling station. But in parts of Arizona you can ride a horse or even a car from dawn till dusk and not see a sign of human habitation. As a New Yorker you are accustomed to living very close to about 8,000,000 other New Yorkers. Those millions touch elbows day and night. They crowd into trains, buses, cars, theaters, stores, apartments, in an anthill existence. But many a family in Arizona has no neighbor within five, twenty-five, sometimes even fifty miles. This is not to argue that one way of life is "better" than the other. Or — is it? Truly, isn't it "better" to be intimate with trees and mountains than with sky-scrapers and taxis? With a few relaxed, casual, friendly people than with a crush of charged-up, nervous, pill-gulping, martini-sipping multitudes?

New York City has "canyons" created by streets of sky-scrapers. But Nature's own Grand Canyon in Arizona forces us to think in far broader scope. "If all the people who have ever lived on earth could be gathered, they would easily fit into a box one mile long by one mile wide by one mile high," wrote Hendrik Willem Van Loon, the great historian. "And that big box could then be dropped into just one tiny branch of the Grand Canyon and be lost forever." Thus he impressed us, accurately, with how small mankind really is, compared to the sheer spaciousness of the West.

Today's visitor is overwhelmed when he reaches Kansas; wheat fields stretch over the horizon, then on and on, and on, and on forever! When he comes to that first great barrier, the Rocky Mountains, his excitement mounts quickly, for the New Yorker can climb a slope and see a whole wilderness world at his feet. Remembering publicity on the Lost Dutchman Gold Mine, he can, and often does, hurry on southward to Arizona's mysterious

2

old Superstition Mountain, climb up nearly a mile, find no nuggets but see a richer treasure — a hundred miles of "purple mountain majesties above the fruited plain." Such an adventure is not merely physical, it is spiritual. If you are a person of great emotional intensity you will respond beyond your finest dreaming. And there are hundreds of spots in Arizona where the adventure can be re-lived again and again.

Space, then, is the first great discovery made by the newcomer. And if this be truly the blessed region of room-enough, it seems even more so because of what's overhead. One characteristic of the West (most portions) is that it gets relatively little rain. Remember that line in the beloved song "Home On The Range" — "And the skies are not cloudy all day"? It is based on fact. Out here in the West the sun isn't just vaguely above us, it shines! Many towns in Arizona boast, accurately, that it shines at least 360 days in every year.

The open sky, then, enhances the feeling of spaciousness. "The great blue dome of the West," somebody has called it. Gray days are relatively few; azure days, turquoise days, are routine. Again, this is not always "good," but to newcomers it at least is surprising. In some areas the cloudless days are too many, with the result that heat and drouth scorch the land, yet even there they add to the feeling of unlimited space.

Westerners are very proud of their sun and sky and open spaces. Their chambers of commerce advertise these attractions endlessly, and with reason; good weather and good scenery attract paying guests. Tourism — the thousands of resort towns, hotels, motels, cafes, and guest ranches — is a major industry. Of all the vacation areas in America the sunny parts of the West are most popular, with Arizona near the top. That abiding sunshine enables people from the icy North and East to play here in shirt sleeves even in January.

Many of the tourists come with eager open minds so that they quickly see opportunities for business. They stay to become merchants, resort operators, mining executives, bankers, manufacturers, farmers, ranchers, doctors, lawyers, teachers. And so the population of the state is growing at almost appalling rate; authorities who study such things say that Phoenix may be the biggest city in the world before the year 2060. (In 1967 the Phoenix population was crowding toward 700,000.)

Another big influence is history, or folklore; the "Wild West" legend is famous in every corner of the globe now. Arizona's open space is room for drama on colossal scale, its plains and valleys are stages, its mountains and canyons are scenic wings, its sun a spotlight for all. Romance-loving easterners come out smiling and eager to see this great theater and become a part of its action. Who can blame them? They are to be respected for reaching toward a life that seems inspired.

Whatever their reasons for coming, people are seldom disappointed. That lure of the West has been strong for more than two centuries, and in approaching the 1970's seems stronger than ever. Much of it is intangible, something we can't touch or measure or put in the bank or even express very clearly. But it is a powerful force, it stimulates our emotions, our heart interest, by seeming to promise us a better life. Many philosophers and writers have tried to express that heart feeling about the West and a few have done so with skill. Among the best of them was Sharlot Hall. As a girl of twelve she was a horse wrangler for her father's wagons when he brought his family out of the East into the setting sun. Later she became Arizona's poet laureate, and in one matchless poem caught the spirit of our region as it was then and is today:

4

# AWAY OUT WEST

Away, away from city and street;
Away from the tread of thronging feet
That hurry and crowd, but never know
The trails where man may joy to go.
Away where the pines are green and tall,
And skies are blue and high hills call.
Away from the things that cry and clamor,
And beat on the heart like an iron hammer —
The needless needs that chain the soul
In a ceaseless round to a useless goal.
Away where the stars are big and bright
As lamps of God in the desert night;
When silence lies like a waveless sea
That reaches from now to eternity —
Till dawn comes up on the peaks above
Like the light of joy in the eyes you love.
Away where the earth is strong and free,
With room for the men who are yet to be;
Where hope is truest and life is best —
    Away out West.

Out from the things that cramp and hold,
And shape man's life in an iron mold.
Out from walls on every side;
Out to the spaces clean and wide;
Sky for roof and earth for floors;
Home as big as all outdoors;
Wind in the pines for a singing harp,
Campfire high on a granite scarp;
Rustling soft in the leaves and grass,
Shy and quick where the wild things pass;

5

Life of the wilderness, better to meet
Than the things of night on a city street.
Out where we turn from yesterday
And wash our hearts in the clean today.
Out where a man is free to make
New roads of life for new hope's sake —
Free to dream of the greater man
He meant to be when life began;
Where the soul has room for its highest quest —
    Away out West.

West of the lands where life is old,
Choked by the dust till its blood is cold;
Dull and dumb with toil and fret;
Numb with the pain of old regret;
Dead men's hopes and memories
That whisper and call in every breeze;
Dead men's work and dead men's bones
That clog the earth and crowd the stones;
Till the heart is hushed and the pulse goes still
Lest it wake the dead and cross their will.
West, O West, where the sun each day
Bids the feet to be up and away;
Where new trails run and new lands wait,
And a man and God are his only fate.
Where the far blue peaks and the valleys wide
Cleanse the heart of its hasty pride,
And the open sky and boundless space
Carve something great on the poorest face;
Where a man's on honor to be his best —
    Away out West.

## 2. *Under The Sun*

By "Arizona sun country," then, we mean simply those lands mastered and shaped by sunshine — which is the source of all light and color and life; simply our vast expanse which, under the constant play of sun and shadow, may distill terrifying majesty, or infinite calm. Sun is our one constant among fantastic variations; overacting like a child, sometimes moody, sometimes cruel, always aggressive, the sun paints here with its most lavish brush.

Our Arizona sun affects routine to a degree inconceivable back east. The happy hired girl in my home — she sings Sonoran love songs while she slowly works — takes a basket of wet laundry to the clothesline, hangs it, and refills the basket with clothes she hung out just thirty minutes before, this in January as well as July. She uses no bluing, no fancy bleaching powders, no chemical antiseptics; from those few minutes in the sun, shirts and sheets return dazzling white. She would be offended at the thought of a hot-air dryer operated by electricity or gas.

I am writing this by an open upstairs window, at 10:15 A.M. on February 4. In the patio below me my grandchildren romp — in sun suits; Robin and Erin, Randy and Davey and Ricky, Sharie and Wendy with their doll buggies, Larry the toddler. They are Caucasian; all-American Irish-German-Scotch-English-French — a marvelous blood mixture. But they look much like carefree little Mexicans with their skins of creamy tan, and they will never show that anemic paleness so noticeable on children from the East. What's more, these sun-bathed children suffer relatively few head colds. The desert is a boon to all who suffer from respiratory diseases, arthritis, rheumatism, hay fever, and many other ailments, including mental illnesses. It lolls the sufferer into taking a rest, into complete relaxation, into forgetting his worries and fears, replacing these with new interests and hopes.

We have long since learned to dress sensibly in Arizona. True, Phoenix and Tucson have become two of the fashion centers of the

7

world, yet neither our men nor women put on clothes beyond the point of comfort and health. My Adele and I attend a church of three thousand members, a magnificent temple with great pipe organ, distinguished choir, and formality dripping from the high vaulted ceiling. Yet many a time I have seen beloved ministers in their shirt sleeves, sport shirts even in the pulpit, and if a summer worshiper shows up in a coat we hasten to greet him, knowing he is a new-comer to town. Formal dress at our summer parties may mean white shirt clipped at the elbows and open at the neck. This shocks the pseudo-sophisticate from out of state, until he gradually climbs to our plateau of good will and intelligence.

In desert Arizona, football games are played at night to escape the sun's sure intensity. But we play golf and go swimming and play tennis every afternoon of the year. We bask at patio tables, under those gorgeously colorful umbrellas, while we enjoy February lunch. Once in a while — but rarely — the sky darkens and it rains, or tries to, for perhaps as much as forty-eight hours, and after the first day of it we are amusingly depressed; we have to remind ourselves that in Seattle or Houston or St. Louis or Milwaukee or Pittsburgh or Brooklyn the sky may stay continuously gray for forty-eight days.

Jealous regions, notably Florida and California, sometimes ask the world archly, "Just how hot does it get in summer in southern Arizona?"

"It gets so hot," our natives will tell you, "that when our coyotes chase jackrabbits, both walk."

They are sensible animals. And they set the pace for us sensible human beings. I have personally measured 140 degrees Fahrenheit by placing a thermometer on the desert sand at 2 P.M. in August, and the thermometer in the shade of my patio porch has touched 112 degrees. Such extremes of course would kill people in humid climes. Our heat parches, but it does not depress; the desert air is somehow thin and can be breathed without gasping; perspiration is markedly less and energies do not sag nearly so quickly as in the horrid torrid stretches of the mid-West, the East and the South. I have lived in

8

those areas — and I dearly love the people there — but believe me, this desert heat is much more endurable than theirs. Our relative freedom from dampness is worth what little extra discomfort extra degrees of temperature bring.

We have, in addition, fought back at those temperatures with singular success in the field of science. Remember, our desert rainfall is only six or seven inches a year. This very dryness enabled us, about 1930, to develop a marvelous mechanism for our comfort, an evaporative cooler, a box with walls of wet excelsior and a fan or blower inside. This cooler sucks hot air through the wet excelsior, drops its temperature from 110 to 80 degrees, and blows it into our houses. It costs less than $100 to install and less than $3 a month to operate, hence even our humblest homes and work shacks can enjoy them. Yet even that marvelous evaporative cooler is obsolescent because our scientists have perfected refrigeration for houses and cars. Almost no home today costing over $8,000 is built without refrigeration, and virtually every office, factory, store, theater, and church has it.

One other weapon against heat must be mentioned. Time was when only the rich, and not many of them, dared try to own a private swimming pool. Back yonder forty years or so a city might have a "natatorium" — remember? — where mother or father might take the children, say once or twice in summer, as a memorable treat. But in Phoenix, Tucson, and other Arizona desert communities today, a pool is almost as much a necessity of life as is the television set. Take a low plane ride over residential Phoenix; many subdivisions show pools in 80 per cent of the back yards, of homes costing no more than $10,000. Foolish luxury? Not at all. The health and recreational value of that pool is worth all it costs. Its only burden is keeping the leaves and the bees and the neighboring dogs and children out.

Most of our desert-zone gardening is done in autumn and winter. As early as September 15, I plant ranunculus and anemone bulbs, African daisies, Iceland poppies, sweet peas, nasturtiums, petunias, snapdragons, stock, or any of a dozen other fine flowers, knowing they will be in lavish bloom shortly after Christmas, and on into late May. By September my Adele and I are enjoying limeades from the beautiful lime tree in our patio. From October through June we eat the fruit from our own lemon, orange, tangerine, and grapefruit trees. We do not envy our cousins in the cold East. As a writer I can live anywhere — I need only a typewriter and a desk — and Adele and I have traveled world-wide, lived long stretches in other climes. We prefer life here under the sun.

## II.  THE NEW AND ENJOYABLE LIFE

One recent winter day a shiny limousine threaded cautiously through the cactus and chaparral of the Arizona desert and stopped beside a red cliff. A butler got out, set up a card table with two chairs and cushions, then held open the door. A middle-aged lady and gentleman, obviously wealthy New Yorkers, stepped out and moved to the chairs. Both of them relaxed as visibly as kittens in the sun while their manservant cooked lunch on a small gasoline stove and served them. Manservant, master, and mistress were all aristocratic, and charming; all were awed by the strange beauty of the wilderness.

These facts I know because I was sun-dozing on top of the red cliff beside which their car was parked, and when they had finished with their lunch I couldn't resist the urge to climb down and crash their party. We powwowed until six that evening, when I cooked supper for all of us over a cow-chip fire.

Those folks came out to the Southwest for a month's vacation at a resort hotel. But they have never been back to New York; not once. The gentleman has closed out his eastern business by mail and become a cattle rancher, a breeder of fancy stock. He also owns part interest in two mines and an orange grove. The greenest possible

11

dudes when I met them, all three dress, act, and talk differently now. They don't wear buckskin, walk bowlegged, or call you "Podnuh," but they have joined and are enthusiastic members of a significant new clan of Americans.

The clan is dedicated to the proposition that the region along the Mexican border not only can support human life, but can actually enrich it. This is revolutionary. The 1849'ers reported the region as one terrific hell of heat and hunger, and until about 1900 it was regarded by most outsiders as a zone to be avoided by all but fugitives and the most courageous of adventurers. Even until 1920 or so, most people who "went to Arizona" were suspected of being either tuberculars or screwballs.

Whatever changed that feeling, I wouldn't know, unless it was the eventual pooling up of counter-propaganda from us screwballs. A large percentage of us would dress up fit to kill, visit back east, and make it clear that we had abundant money and no ulcers. We'd mention the endless coveys of quail and doves that came literally into our back yards, tell about the 12-prong buck we shot last autumn, about the rainbow trout we take out of the Arizona streams and lakes, about the armloads of roses we pick in our yards on January 1. Easterners can stand just so much of that kind of talk, then they get wistful. Pretty soon they get jealous; or envious. In the 1930's they started running out here in droves; the war and the peacetime travel boom further stimulated them, so that by 1967 the run looked like a stampede.

People by the astonishing thousands are deliberately settling on the same dry-and-dangerous land that awed the covered-wagon folk. With few exceptions, moreover, they are a vigorous stock, and they are prospering. "The desert is only one to four hours from anywhere now," said one new enthusiast. "It is no longer a place of exile far, far away. It is a Garden, a Land of Opportunity, a Last Frontier, a Region of Romance, a Place of Beneficent Beauty."

He sounded like a chamber-of-commerce secretary of the old school, but he is a wealthy Bostonian building himself a mansion on

12

the sunny side of Squaw Peak. He is fifty-seven and says he is going to retire. His retirement may last six months, but I would bet against it. John C. Lincoln, who founded and developed Cleveland's Lincoln Electric Company, came out one winter and bought a desert home and a rocking chair. He sat for two months, then got up and built one of Arizona's — and possibly America's — finest resort hotels, near his home. George Borg — Mr. Clutch — came to the desert to retire in a quiet cottage, and instead developed a dude resort now worth about a million dollars. Down the same road in Paradise Valley — which is an apt name, once you've felt the spell of the area — Fowler McCormick of farm-implement wealth developed one of America's most spectacular ranch enterprises. His sudden "hobby" interest there helped boom dollar-an-acre desert land to ten-thousand-dollar-an-acre land, with plenty of takers. Burridge Butler, Chicago radio-station owner and magazine publisher, came to the desert to get away from publishing and radio, but soon bought another magazine and radio station, both Arizona products. Clarence Budington Kelland, one of America's most famous authors, was traveling from New York to California's Elysian fields and got sidetracked on the Arizona desert. Amazingly, not a darn soul rushed up to beg for his autograph. No one bothered to lionize him, no one begged him to read a manuscript or make a speech. He canceled out his California trip and bought a desert ranch. He later wrote half a dozen Arizona novels — thus becoming our number-one press agent — was head of our Republican party, and lured out literally dozens of other eastern men of influence.

Such folk, it is revealed if you prod them, have an innate distaste for Hollywood — Hollywood being not a place, but a state of mind, one which is nonexistent on the desert. Bob Hope comes over often to play golf, and we have trouble collecting a committee to greet him. When Sinatra comes, he has to do his own swooning. When Gary Cooper stalked down our Central Avenue, we stared a little, maybe said, "Hiya, Gary," then passed on.

Not all our new settlers are famous or distinguished or rich.

13

Not all are middle-aged or old; indeed, the majority are under forty. But all seem to have that certain something inside them; they are happy to match wits with a tough he-man region. A century ago they would have been the organizers and captains of the wagon trains. I have done some polling among them recently. The individual is a little haughty, proud, self-assured. This, I hold, is a priceless thing of the spirit — something bred in folk and nurtured by environment, the true "American strain." Their youngsters climb mountain peaks that have defied us old-timers. Their young marrieds open businesses of their own, rather than merely hunt jobs. They can stand spread-legged on a cliff, look out across fifty or a hundred miles of uninhabited desert, and people it with dreams, then step down and make the dreams come true.

I have seen Indians staring at the strange spectacle of bulldozers leveling landing strips where no paleface had ever been before. From one such airfield, isolated in a country of crimson canyons, I brought home dinosaur tracks molded in rock. An opportunist from back east had cut a road into there and built not only a home but a hotel, and it is full of guests who motor or fly in. Here they can escape from something, yet without a sense of cowardly flight.

Most of the new folks, it develops, are escapists of one sort or another. Pin them down and they frankly admit they are running from the rigors of cold and of city life. "I was Minnesota born and reared," one typical ex-G.I. said. "I had fully expected to go into business there, and I never realized what sub-zero winters meant because I knew nothing else. War training gave me eleven months on the desert. Now I have my wife and baby in a desert cottage and I drive ten miles a day to work. Soon I am going to open a little desert business of my own. If necessary, we'll be poor here; I'd rather be poor here than a multimillionaire back there."

The naked fact is that people are moving west, and southwest; you can verify it via the U. S. Census Bureau, which is constantly estimating and checking. In Phoenix and Tucson you can find young G. I. couples by the thousands who echo the sentiments of that

14

Minnesota lad. They account for the fact that the population of Phoenix, for instance, is now far above half a million, that while suburban two-room apartments are available at $100 per month, many of them rent for $150 and up, and that the union scale for bricklayers is considerably higher than the average union wage for persons engaged in the building trades in the United States.

This younger group — the ones with less money than Lincoln and Borg and Kelland, et al — are imbued with a terrific pioneering urge. They don't seem to demand ease, but rather to seek the conditioning that hard work brings. Which, if I read history right, is a good thing. Nevertheless, we old desert conservatives sometimes view with alarm.

"How can all these strangers make a living here?" I asked a learned friend of mine not long ago. "The desert cities have no factories to speak of, or other big industries. We have no oil boom, no mining boom, no farming except limited irrigation."

He explained that, of America's 200,000,000 people, at least two million have the money to come to the desert and live the remainder of their lives *without* working. Many will continue to receive pay from their eastern businesses. But most important is the way people beget wealth. Those who come here are "successful" types. Their combined brain power is inconceivable, and the desert has endless opportunities for such as they. Remember that recreation alone is one of America's greatest industries, and that the Arizona desert with its mountains and canyons and health-giving warmth is absolutely the best area for recreation ever discovered.

That last may be open to argument, but not much, and is a point of view shared by important thousands. Usually such people are those we like to call rugged individualists. They respond to the sun-country environment. Not all are refined. Indeed, many are tough; yet they are self-reliant and therefore admirable. I know one family — Stephen Ragsdale is the pappy's name — who pioneered on the desert fifty miles from the nearest settlement. Absolutely nothing in the way of opportunity was visible to any normal human

15

being, yet these good folks stuck it out and became wealthy there. The children drove an old jalopy a hundred miles a day in order to finish high school. The pappy was, for my money, a brilliant thinker. He had to be. He was a tough-acting old fellow with a heart of gold, and he had to be that, too.

Yet another acquaintance, much younger, commutes sixty miles each day from his desert-wilderness home to operate a business in our city. Is he happy? I wouldn't answer that categorically, but I do know that he netted better than $90,000 in the past seven years, that he has three children who motor in to school and own their own horses, that he is married to the same woman he started with, that he loves to sing and whistle and throw barbecue parties and pitch horseshoes.

I rode out with this friend one night last week to "spend a night among the rattlesnakes." He stopped the car suddenly in the forest of giant cactus growths. A stag and five does were on our right. In our car lights, they flowed across the road and on away — a moment of unforgettable beauty. Neither of us moved for a minute or two, and then my friend started the car and we drove slowly on through the darkness. Then he said, "You know, Oren, I have never been in a night club."

Several years ago, I spent a day with Harold Bell Wright in his desert home out from Tucson, and I asked him why he lived away out there. "Because," said he, "in spring I literally cannot walk without crushing wild flowers. And because every person you encounter out here seems like a hero or heroine for a novel." He knocked off quite a fortune by writing desert stories, as did his contemporary, Zane Grey. Both men have been dead for years, but John Public generally doesn't care, and so their books keep on selling. The most popular volume in the big Phoenix Public Library, the one in most constant demand, is not some high-toned book-club selection. It is a horse-opera libretto entitled *Riders of the Purple Sage,* by Mr. Grey, in which this man and his girl meet on the desert, see, and go on from there . . . . .

16

It was Grey who unwittingly put his finger right on one secret of the desert's pull. He recognized it as a setting for human drama, fictional or real — drama not of the stodgy, conventional, or moody kind, but of picturesque and audacious derring-do. He said that the desert is a stage for the finest human acting, by which he meant achievement; he predicted the face lifting which has come.

All our now many resort hotels rate sunshine, "open country," and wildlife as their most valuable assets. It is chamber-of-commercial to remind you again that we play golf and tennis all winter, that I can loaf in my patio in shirt-sleeves while you in Chicago or New York are gloomy with January snow. But it is also true, and negotiable. We sell it to you easterners, just as we sell you the facts of our fascinating flora and fauna. Our cacti are eternally popular. Our giant saguaro especially is an awesome creation. It will blossom and bear edible fruit every year for as many as four years without one drop of rain or any help from man. One of my grandchildren has a desert pet that is covered with horns and spits blood from its eyes — a species of horned lizard, harmless and dainty. On a vacant lot near us live diminutive "kangaroos" six inches high, which hop about on their hind legs under the moon. In the yards of our street, and everywhere on the desert, lives a bird that resembles a skinny guinea and that eats rattlesnakes and chases golf balls.

A fantasy land, then; a region of believe-it-or-nots; a country where people just have to act unconventionally. Inevitably, it attracts those with imagination. Inevitably, too, it attracts some who become professional braggarts — sun-country boors who come here, then deride the homes they deserted. They are no more popular here than they were in Bangor or Boston or Milwaukee; they are not accepted here, and fortunately they soon shut down or drift on. So, too, do we freeze out the transient ne'er-do-well element that is forever shifting bases, attracted always by the promise of warm climate and easy living.

The rest stay and share their talents. I think of Frank Lloyd Wright, who probably was America's most distinguished architect.

17

He reached fame in the East, then discovered our desert and adopted it. His Taliesin West — a home and architectural school on the slope of a rocky Arizona desert mountain — was startling in design when he built it a few years ago. But today literally hundreds of our new structures are showing its influence. Suburban architecture in Arizona in time may be recognized as the most artistic in the nation, as well as the most logical, and the most appropriate.

Similarly, easterners with high I. Q.s have recently created symphonic music for our citizens of Scorpion Gulch. Artists of distinction have discovered the desert's rare coloration and light. And in literature — well, when I set out to name those who, I know, have done some of their finest work in Arizona — those in addition to Kelland, Harold Bell Wright, and Grey — the list seems practically endless. It includes every favorite I can think of from Stewart Edward White to Erskine Caldwell, who married an Arizona University coed, through Carl Sandburg, J. B. Priestley, and Willa Cather. Money, then, plus courage and culture, are the assets for our newcomers.

Exactly what all this means for the future of America as a whole I wouldn't dare say. I can't even promise that the desert will enhance your happiness if you move out here. Indeed, I warn you not to move without a preliminary trip for reconnoitering, because you might not fit in. All I know is that I catch the mounting excitement, and I'm thrilled to be part of it, because a million newcomers are suddenly changing the face and feel of the desert. And they're changing it right now, in my time, after it lay virtually unchanged for a million years.

# III. HOW TO LIVE WITH THE SUN

In the opening chapters here I have done what comes naturally, I have praised the Arizona sunshine, implying that it is a beneficence the year round. Now in all fairness I must retreat a bit, issue a warning and offer some tested guidance. For the truth is, our sun is like many other pleasant things in life: enjoyable and beneficial if taken in moderation, but dangerous if taken to excess. Common sense must enter into the matter if we are to enjoy *summer's* ingratiating smile. Surprisingly, this applies more to the natives and old residents than to persons who have just arrived.

Your first move is simply to indoctrinate all for whom you are responsible including, surely, yourself. You'd think we'd all *know* summer has been coming around for quite a while now, and in Arizona with unique potency. Yet we still forget that kids can't just plunge out of school, and adults can't just plunge out of home, hotel or office, with winter skins exposed in fashionable play suits, and not get some prompt reactions. Half the trouble from heat stacks up in May and June. Virtually all of it is unnecessary.

Take your sunshine ten minutes the first morning, ten more that afternoon, and increase it ten minutes twice a day until you are tan. It's as simple as that, and it's your doctor's prescription. Simple?

Look around you about June 1; the streets will be cluttered with pink simpletons! And don't flatter yourself that you are he-man or outdoor-woman enough to ignore that basic precaution. Millions try to, and whine the loudest when their blisters burst.

Our very best doctors warn us that even though you have a protective coat of tan you still face grave danger. Bare heads, bare backs, bare midriffs, bare thighs, are invitations to trouble. We do tend to go naked in Phoenix, Scottsdale, Mesa, Yuma, Tucson, etc., and up to a point it's fun, but beyond that point either the police or the hospital will get you. You aren't even safe under a poolside umbrella or tree, for the intense reflections can still strike you; some light covering is imperative. One of those cute-and-sassy straw hats which cost four times what they ought to because they have dolls dangling from the crown, can be as valuable in preventing skin cancer as in attracting the opposite sex. Some high-quality "sunburn lotion" is a necessity if you are going to run around semi-nude.

The lotions must be studied. More than half of them are worthless except to enrich the manufacturer. I could name two or three that are priceless. What *do* doctors recommend here? Well, phone yours and see. Phone your doctor rather than ask the cute clerk in the drugstore. Phone your *skin* doctor, if you have been sunning more and enjoying it less.

If you are doomed to stay in town, under a roof, you can still win. Just don't eat so confounded much; but don't try to subsist on cocktails and cokes, either. Lighter foods, well balanced, is your cue, plus a deliberate cut-down on physical activity. This, again, is straight from the physician's mouth. It is also common sense, but that's our most uncommon commodity.

Avoid that old fallacy of the cold shower. Do not plunge, sweaty, into lake or pool. Do not allow your hot children to leap under a spraying hose. The gradual approach does it more safely. The tepid bath is more cooling than the cold one. Grandmother told us that, but she — hah! — was an old fogey. Only thing is, the modern scientists have completed long, hard research that proved

20

her right. You may not die from a cold plunge every day, or indeed from heavy eating and hard working and long sunning. But you will debilitate yourself so that by August you'll almost wish you were dead. Or you'll be so irritable that your friends and family will wish you were.

Refreshed by sleep, you'll always have the zip to face a sizzling day. Thus the home refrigeration units and evaporative coolers, already described, have been a godsend to southern Arizona. The "evaps" were pioneered here. No, truth is they were used in India and other places centuries ago, when mothers hung wet blankets over doorways to cool any vagrant breeze. And our own Indians knew enough to put wet cloths on their heads. But the "cooler," the hideous window-box thing that still drips from many an Arizona wall, is a local invention. There is considerable argument about who built the first one, but God bless him, whoever he was. For some of us can Remember When.

And I do mean When. When we had *nothing* to take the edge off the home temperature. Fans? What good were they? The air inside was hot, the fan simply made blast-furnace force. Some of us, clever we, did buy 100-pound cakes of ice, put them in tubs in the living room and turn fans on them. One man I knew rolled his cot up close to his refrigerator, took the butter and milk out, and poked his head right in the open door for the night. But unfortunately refrigerators were new then, too, just being developed from the old ice-box. That one couldn't stand the gaff of a night-long performance with open door. It turned loose a kitchen full of gas. The man had a lovely funeral.

We slept, then, by wetting our sheets at 8 P.M. and spreading them over the mattresses. Their drying process took most of the heat out of the mattresses; until our bodies put it back in. We slept naked — you have heard about Arizona's population explosion, haven't you? At times, and I mean often and by the hundreds, we'd sleep naked on our lawns, even in our front yards if we suspected a breeze might be there. This is no exaggeration; ask any morning-

21

paper boy or milkman of the 1900 to 1930 period. We faced the facts of heat realistically. So must you in your time here.

In each period, the pounding actinic rays of the sun have had marked effect on our social structure, our habit patterns. We weren't as competitive back in the B. C. (Before Coolers) years, so we didn't move as fast. We *ambled* through summer. Before horseless carriages we simply let the horse stand in the shade and fan gnats with his tail until an imaginary cooling set in about 6 P.M., then we'd drive over to friends' house for iced tea and conversation. None of this zipping up and down the boulevards in racy red convertibles; that annoyance (to us sedate folk) didn't strike the town until after coolers did. Back there, people had time. Time to amble. Time to talk and josh about the heat. "The jackrabbits are carrying umbrellas again," we'd say, with twinkling eye. If a fellow asked if you thought it would rain, you were honor-bound to reply "If it don't it'll sure be a long dry spell." That was clever repartee, highly sophisticated, circa 1910.

All in all, those old boys and gals lived with the heat more intelligently than we do. In our day we are so confounded impatient we just won't wait to get protectively browned. It can be very rewarding just to lounge on the chaise longue. That thing, by the way, is pronounced *shay long,* not *chase lounge.* It's a cross between a wheelbarrow and a cot, thus is convenient to move from tree to tree around the pool or yard. Lounging in it, even when the house is refrigerated, is a God's blessing. You can let down, there; let your nerves sag, your temper relax.

Our pools, too, deserve some serious consideration.

Time was when all we Valley of the Sun folk had was a canal. Then Phoenix got Riverside Pool and we figured we were metropolitan. Many more public pools exist now, and Phoenix has more home patio pools than any other city of its size in the world. Truly you can cool off in a pool.

But etch this indelibly on your mind: *Your attitude toward any body of water bigger than a bucketful can save or cost your life.*

Thousands have been drowned in bathtubs. Water is a clutching arm of death even for persons not in swimming. It is especially imperative that we cultivate a healthy hydrophobia in our children. It is impossible to over-emphasize the danger, and almost as impossible to break through public indifference to it. I have interviewed a dozen or more safety experts on this, and from them have gotten a priceless 7-point program of protection, applicable in Arizona and everywhere else in the world:

1. *Learn to swim.* Now don't shrug, or smirk in boredom. Incredible numbers of us don't know how, and thousands more think they know yet don't. True, this is fundamental; but it's also true that we ignore it. See that every member of your family knows.

2. *NEVER SWIM ALONE.* That's in big type for emphasis. Never, no never, swim alone, no matter how expert you are; your very confidence can kill you. The Buddy System — at least one friend near you at all times — is the surest safety measure, well tested. Even a friend who can't swim can hold out a pole, a towel, a piece of clothing, and save a life. Never swim alone is the most important water warning.

3. *Do not be a show-off.* You have all seen the juvenile mind (though he may be well along in years) who thinks it's funny to rock the boat, defy the rapids, push people into the pool, *ad lib ad nauseam.* It would be a blessing if he alone *did* drown, we can reason. And well he may. But unfortunately, he may take us with him. Beat his brains out verbally, the moment he starts his show.

4. *Never ride in any boat that will not float upside down.* One of the strangest phenomena in our Valley of the Sun is the fact that this waterless desert region is overflowing with boating buffs. All year our highways to the lakes will stream with trailers. Too many of the boats on them will sink if capsized.

23

All metal boats should have sealed air chambers. Never get into one that doesn't have. Then if the boat tips over, *cling to it,* without struggling, until help comes or you float it to shore. Just hold a hand on it to keep your nose out of water. That's all you need.

*5. Do not put your trust in "life preservers."* Thousands of us feel that the mere presence of life belts, floater cushions, or similar devices is protection enough. "You can't swim? So what? We have cushions that will float." So you step blithely in, the motor roars, and your stupid host zooms you out to the middle of the deep lake. There, towing a skiing beauty, he swerves and capsizes. You scream in terror. You do surface, but that cushion suddenly is fifteen yards away. Now you complete the picture.

*6. Don't neglect your children.* Well *really,* you may exclaim here; how unnecessary a warning! But hold on, madam, or sir. The sad record shows that the warning is anything but silly. People by the thousands do neglect their offspring; people just like you, in Arizona.

One year little Linda Mears's mother dozed off beside their pool. They had to bury Linda. Almost every week, year round, we read of a child's drowning in her own patio pool. You can't even trust a paid lifeguard at a public pool; he is usually an over-muscled, sexed-up gent from high school or college, bored with being your baby sitter. (That's not quite fair; some are thoroughly responsible. But many aren't.) Never frighten your child, building a morbid fear of water, but do force a deep respect for water's danger, and do enforce these strict safety rules. Arizona sun lulls us into carelessness. Be wary.

*7. If you fall into water, do not panic.* Hysteria is the result of being unprepared, so — be prepared. That's what these seven rules are for. The famed Boy Scout motto is one reason why the Scouts have the best water safety record of any organization in the nation. Incidentally, the Scouts pioneered the Buddy System. Prepare

24

your own mind, then talk the matter out with your loved ones. The discussion itself will prevent most of the trouble, for it focuses attention on what not to do. So, keep cool in the water, figuratively as well as literally; cool and collected — and safe.

One more good trick remains to help you outwit the desert summer sun. It too is "obvious" and shouldn't need recording, yet for every new generation it is new. It is simply this: summer is the time to read.

"Read? Nobody reads any more!"

Oh, don't they! More magazines are published now than ever before, more books are being sold than at any other time in history, with teen-agers — of all people — reading the most. And after all, you yourself have repeatedly said that summer television is banal; and that you *ought* to read more and wish you had time for it.

Well then. Now's the golden moment. The book stores are bulging. So are the libraries. Four or five good novels, five or six good fact books, and before you realize it school time will be here again, you will have forgotten the heat problem, and be charged with energy for the new season.

\* \* \*

Now, this chapter is primarily a guidance for those who must stay in the hot zones. But you are not to conclude that *all* of Arizona is like that in summer. Keep in mind the incomparable beauties and summer comfort in the White Mountains, the matchless scenery in the area from Ft. Apache to McNary, for example; and the Alpine region, the wonderful fishing country around Diamond Rock and dozens of other spots. Perhaps most noteworthy of all is the drive from Alpine to Clifton over the Coronado Trail. And you can "freeze" at the Grand Canyon in July!

In these fine areas the sun is tamed by altitude. Go there and enjoy them.

# IV.  DESERT SPRING SONG

The very essence of showmanship is surprise; suddenly doing, saying, or revealing the unexpected. That fact makes our Arizona desert the Number One showplace of America. You who are accustomed to moist fields and woodlands quite naturally expect spring to be showy, but you are seldom prepared for what happens in the arid desert zones where "nothing" grows; you cannot envision the contrast between August and April. But nowhere else in the world is the springtime miracle of resurrection more astonishing or more inspiring. Between Sundays in March or April, the whole desert universe can change.

"It is impossible, but true, that I walk today on a Persian carpet of 10,000 acres, patterned so thick with flowers that every step crushes them."

That was part of an Easter message from a famous Arizona desert dweller beloved by millions of Americans. Nor was he exaggerating. He walked in incredible beauty. Not just buds popping, a crocus there, a dogwood here, a few shy violets peeking around logs; those famed flowers are wonderful, but they would become lost in the desert's profusion. Nature somehow made the desert a laboratory in which to do almost everything in extreme.

These desert flowers are shoe high and are *everywhere*. Most individual blossoms are the size of silver dollars, but many are smaller than dimes. Some are so small that one match-head size is called jumbo, by hobbyists who make a point of raising them. But that great Mexican maguey which looms on yonder horizon is forty-three feet tall, which is more than a four-story building! And that cluster of yuccas — Candles of the Lord, the natives say — are taller than men on horseback. The giant saguaro cactus, standing like a sentinel all over southern Arizona, sometimes is fifty feet tall. Its blossoms — the official state flower — crown its leafless "arms," a glory to behold. The bisnaga or barrel cactus, the prickly pear, the deerhorn, these and many more (there are at least six hundred species of cactus alone on our desert regions) flaunt splashes of color when spring is on the loose. And yet, strangers normally never suspect them of blooming at all.

When you come to enjoy the flowers you will want a camera, especially one equipped for color work. If you are something of a botanist you can have a memorable field day. Golden poppies probably will impress you first. One happy tourist discovered his while looking — of all things! — for lost gold. He had driven to Arizona's famed Superstition Mountain where the Lost Dutchman Mine is said to conceal fabulous millions, and as he circled a cliff into Peralta Canyon, there lay the gold!

It was what miners call a "surface outcropping," truly. Rains and warmth had combined just right here, and so the poppy blossoms were splashed all over the valley, up the slope of the canyon, and even on parts of the south walls. It was as if some gigantic smelter had tilted a ladle to pour out molten gold, and watched it spread and harden there. It glistened. It was dazzling. It was treasure in incredible profusion.

Not all years are "flower years" in the Southwest, although every season has worth-while exhibits; about once in five, Nature simply goes on a flower stampede, and people from all over this continent go there to enjoy it. You can learn from weather reports

28

or direct from chambers of commerce and travel clubs when the season is going to be "right" in a given vicinity.

The deserts — so called — of Arizona, west Texas, New Mexico, Nevada, Utah, and California, have rainfall of two to eight inches a year. Check that against your home-town record, you who live in the north or east. Thus you can marvel at the desert's wild hollyhocks and daisies; at the lilies, verbena, hyacinth, paintbrush, tulips and primroses, and all the others only a university botanist can name. Whence came they?

Over the centuries, birds have brought in seeds. Bulbs and seeds have been washed onto the lower, dryer zones from the high mountains, where much rain falls. Others are lifted to arid slopes by winds that can come whining like harps of Hades. Then they lurk in the thin surface soil, sometimes for years, waiting for the right combination of February showers and sunshine. When the magic moment arrives, they leap.

Many desert flowers open only in the majesty of night. If you have made friends in, say, Carefree, Arizona, one may telephone you near a sundown in May.

"Come to our home at once," this elated person will urge you. "We have just learned that the Queen is arriving!"

The Queen? Indeed yes, Her Majesty *La Reina de la Noche,* The Queen of the Night. And hers is a royal command, not to be ignored.

You hasten to your friend's garden or perhaps out on the open desert itself, and you will be seated before nothing more impressive than four or five ugly leafless sticks. But this is her throne. On it will be one, or up to fifty, queer balls. These have been watched carefully for days.

"Late this afternoon they showed first sign of cracking," the friend will tell you. "The sun is already out of sight. Within another hour these flower buds will be opening. You can actually watch the movement as petal after petal appears."

Thus it will be for about four or five hours. And by midnight

29

the ugly stalks will be glorious with blossoms as large as salad plates. Each will be white, or creamy, tinted with lavender. And the spicy fragrance from just one plant can be so distinctive and potent that you can sense it sometimes a mile away. You and your party will study it in minute detail, photograph it, sketch it, speculate on the sheer beauty and wonder of it, knowing that it blooms only at night and only one night a year. Next morning its blossoms droop, and are done. Small wonder that the plant holds high place in regional folklore.

Once in the legendary long ago there lived in Mexico a beautiful maiden named Lolita. All the young men were in love with her, but Don Mario wooed her most ardently of all. He came each evening under her balcony to strum his guitar and sing:

> Maiden divine,
> All beauty is yours.
> Beautiful things
> Will I give to thee,
> If thou thyself
> Will only be mine.

But her papa, we are told, was a realist. He strode forth one night, clanking his sabre no doubt, and roared, "My daughter already has everything that is beautiful, young man! What could you bring her more beautiful than I have given her, hah?"

Don Mario was stumped for a moment. Then he accepted the challenge. He rode away and came back with a gift that did, indeed, overwhelm the papa and the maiden alike with its priceless beauty. You've guessed it — he brought a Queen of the Night; and so they were married and lived happily ever after.

More prosaic but hardly less interesting is the root of that Queen. Deep underground she develops a beetlike growth that amounts to a reservoir. Often this weighs 100 to 150 pounds, and rootlets from it grow *upward* to gather whatever little surface rain may fall. If none falls for a year or more, the Queen will still bloom from that reservoir of water and strength.

30

No less phenomenal is that venerable old king of the desert, the giant cactus or sahuaro, which seems defiant of everything. It has no leaves, but it is studded with dangerous stubby thorns. Its inside is spongy, held together by a strong skeleton of perpendicular rods. It is, in truth, a water tank on the desert, drinking in and storing any water it can get, and the average rainfall where it grows is about six inches annually. It is such a camel that it can grow, blossom, bear edible fruit, and defy all the elements, even under very adverse conditions. Normally sahuaros grow about one inch in height a year. They are found only in southern Arizona and northern Mexico — notwithstanding the fact that artists too frequently picture them all the way from Oregon to Louisiana.

The century plant also is spectacular. It does not bloom once in one hundred years, as its name suggests; it may adorn the hillside as a rosette of green daggers for only ten years, then bloom. Actually, its time varies from ten to seventy years. And when it starts, it moves fast. The great central flower stalk will shoot up in a few weeks, sometimes growing as much as a foot in twenty-four hours, resembling a giant asparagus. And after blooming, the whole plant dies. This plant, called also agave and *maguey,* has enjoyed centuries of economic importance to Indians and other natives of the Southwest, besides adorning the landscape with its flowers. It is the source of excellent rope, soap, human food, stock food, and three kinds of drinking liquors, including the fiery *tequila* of Mexico.

The yuccas, or Candles of the Lord, very common in Arizona, also are the state flower of New Mexico, and when you ride from El Paso to Lordsburg in season you pass through literal forests of blossoms. The usual thick trunk of this flower, a true member of the lily family, will be a few inches to a few feet high and possibly branched two or three times. On the end of each fork grows a thick rosette or cluster of leaves about fourteen inches long. These are flat, meaty daggers, and we have named the whole plant Spanish Dagger for them. From the center of that rosette the flower stalk will grow. It may be two feet high, or six. A dense cluster of buds will turn into white blossoms, so thick that one stalk could fill the biggest vase in your home. The individual flower is bell shaped.

Yucca blossoms present one of the strangest examples of co-operation or team work in all of nature. A moth, called Pronuba, carries pollen from one blossom to the other, then lays her eggs in the blossoms to be hatched and nourished there. No other insect helps, no other medium is used. Without Pronuba, yucca could not exist; without yucca, Pronuba could not exist.

Fibres of the yucca stalk and leaves are used by Indians for making baskets, plaques, cord, sandals, mats. Cows learn to nuzzle into the daggers and eat the flowers. But for people, the law says a firm "Hands off." It is in fact illegal, besides being selfish and wasteful, to gather wildflowers anywhere on the desert.

Lord and Lady Halifax, of London, visited Arizona one season and marveled at the profusion of beauty on the desert landscape. "Of all the wild flowers here," said he, "I think the cacti are the most striking. Especially the ocotillo, with its red torch against the sky."

His host hastened to correct him. Ocotillo is not a cactus, even though it is a thorny thing. Yucca and *maguey* also are commonly miscalled cacti. Most strangers apparently think that *all* desert growths belong to the cactus clan. It is a fact, however, that the cacti are showy. Their blossoms last longer, defy cutting because they have no important stems and are guarded by vicious thorns, and they appear in an infinite variety of tints and hues.

Some are delicate yellow, some are in little-sister shades of rose, some thrust up provocative carmine like a siren's lips, many are two-toned and variegated. Wallpaper, dress fabrics, bedspreads and curtains have all been patterned direct from photographs of prickly pear "ears" and blossoms. Some plants, like the bisnaga or barrel cactus, are adorned by a circular crown of blossoms each spring, so perfect as to appear artificial. Every hue of the spectrum can be found in the cactus blooms sometime from February to June. And most, like the sahuaro, prickly pear, and night-blooming cereus, produce delicious fruit. That of the sahuaro has for centuries been a mainstay of food for the desert Indians such as Pimas and Papagos. It is eaten raw — tastes somewhat like a pomegranate or cranberry — and is cooked into a sweet, nourishing kind of concentrate or jam.

Come, therefore, expecting weeks of lazy days and luscious nights in which to enjoy desert flower time. Even the ironwood trees will bloom for you — a delicate purple — and the leafless palo verde — a billowing mass of yellow. You can rest body and soul here as never before. The beauty of all the desert trees and plants are an inspiration. By their sheer audacity and hardiness, as well as their abundance, the desert flowers create an emotional symphony in man quite above that known in the damper wooded zones.

# V. TREASURE IN THE HILLS

Of all the stories that enrich the lore of the Southwest, none equals those fascinating ones that have to do with hidden treasure. And no state offers so many as Arizona.

They are more than legendary. A legend is a half-truth; a bit of history which cannot be entirely documented. Some of our lost gold records are as "pure" as the sunrise itself. Yet some others have indeed been tinted in the re-telling down the years, imagination being what it is. How you separate fact from fiction, then, is a delightful part of the problem. The hard part is going to the actual location of any given treasure, for that involves both sweat and danger.

From half a century of exploration and study I know where about forty of our lost treasures are supposed to be hidden. Many are natural — deposits of silver or gold, once found then lost again. Others are composed of coins and jewels hidden by man himself. But — *where?*

One is within two miles of Weaver's Needle, the central and highest peak in Arizona's mysterious old Superstition Mountain. Another is in leather bags hidden by robbers back behind the Frozen Waterfalls in Colossal Cave, about a mile from the entrance. A third is an olla of golden nuggets "positively" buried near the wall of ancient Tumacacori Mission. Others are scattered like mirages throughout the deserts and plains. I own none of these locations; you may go there and search.

That the treasures work powerfully on man's imagination was brought home to me once at daybreak. I heard excited pounding on my front door. I came down in pajamas. The man at my door spoke almost before I could open up.

"You wrote an article about the Lost Dutchman Mine," he began. "In The Saturday Evening Post."

"Yes."

"I have come to find it," he blurted. "Now you must show me where to start searching."

My visitor had been a furrier in Alsace, until he read my article, then he sold everything to come to Arizona. He was wide-eyed, hypnotized. He had been lured eight thousand miles by a simple bit of regional history.

Six years later he was still searching. We liked him in Arizona. He was a friendly fellow, middle-aged, with eyes that gazed at far horizons, a man who would have sailed with Columbus, or who would have marched with Coronado hunting the Seven Cities of Gold.

I have watched every other human desire melt in the heat of gold fever. Many hopeful ones have come to search, and found only tragedy in the wilderness. When they disappear, or when their bodies are found, the sheriff will tell you that they were victims of thirst, exhaustion, injury, or foul play.

"We were merely tracing down clues in a canyon," Calvin Blaine reported, breathlessly, to the sheriff in my town, "when somebody began shooting at us with a high-powered rifle. We had only a .22 with which to shoot back. We couldn't see him, but he kept us behind rocks until sundown." Nobody ever knew who tried to kill Blaine.

Charles Williams went with his wife on a quiet picnic near one location of legendary treasure, and while she dozed in the winter sun he hiked off up the hill. A blizzard came, and trapped him.

When he didn't return, she went for help. Dozens, then hundreds, of us tramped through the storm trying to find him, without success. Days later he staggered out, half-dead, incoherent. But — in his hand he clutched little sticks of gleaming yellow gold! They were ore concentrates found in a cave, smelted crudely and stored there a century earlier by Spaniards. He said there was more, and many men have searched long months — but never found again the cave Charles Williams found, and lost, in the snow.

My good friend Angelo Mangino, badly overworked, took to the hills a few years ago for recreation. He began bringing home pretty colored stones, picked up here and there. One, the size of a cocoanut, he put on his mantel. Months later a mason repairing the fireplace accidentally knocked the stone off and broke it.

"Sa-a-a-ay!" the man exclaimed. "I used to be a miner. This rock is full of gold!"

It was, too. Assayed, it showed nearly $70,000 to the ton, and ore at $10 a ton can be profitable. But poor Angelo hadn't the faintest idea where he picked up that stone, nor could all our frantic searchings help him.

Dan Williamson, a former judge and state historian in Arizona, showed me five large black marbles one day. Years before, while hunting deer, he had picked them up on a mountainside in the Pinal range, and kept them as souvenirs. Others had been scattered thick in the gravel over an area at least a hundred feet square. Many were as large as eggs. A philosopher, he decided never to tempt fate or his fellow man by revealing where he found them.

In terms of rocks and gleaming nuggets my own adventures haven't been so fruitful. Yet I can't complain. The Dons Club of Phoenix, an earnest group of Arizona historians, commissioned me a while back to prepare a little pamphlet about the Lost Dutchman mine, for a favor at their annual banquet. One hundred copies were ordered, barely enough for the Dons and their wives. But a printer mis-read instructions and turned out a thousand copies. So the Dons, rather foolishly I thought, put the extras on sale. My royalties

37

from several editions, foreign translations, radio, and movie rights have to date exceeded $14,000, and I worked less than two hours writing. So far as I can learn, I am the only person who has acquired any treasure from the mine since the Dutchman himself died.

Try as I will, I haven't been able to repeat such a strike, yet I shall forever have the virus of gold fever coursing through my veins. It is not an unpleasant malady, even though contagious and incurable. J. Frank Dobie of Texas had it. Philip Bailey of California had it. Neither, I'll wager, ever picked up a rock worthy of smelting, but in this Mexican border region each found bonanzas in books about the lost mines.

Old whanghide gents who haven't shaved since Coolidge was President, are likely to be your richest sources of information and your most talented narrators. And too, I know a widowed mother of thirteen, who has a dash of drama in her soul and kinship with the high blue hills. She has spent years hunting lost mines, and found pay dirt enough to support herself and her children. She and others of the clan talk best on their home grounds — say at a campfire in Skeleton Canyon, or halfway up the slope of Squaw Peak, stark in the western sky. Mystics though they are, earthy, uncouth, strange, you'll find them sentimental and sociable as well. Folk such as they have been telling that Lost Dutchman legend since Don Miguel Peralta first worked the mine in the 1840's. So, here's my best-selling legend again:

In old Sonora, Mexico, austere Don Miguel operated a great cattle ranch. His lovely daughter, Rosita, had a lover, Carlos. One night Don Miguel discovered the lovers together, and Carlos was forced to flee. Don Miguel struck a gong that brought his hundreds of armed *vaqueros* running to the patio of his home.

"Hurry, you dullards!" he roared at them. "Bring the swine back to me. With my own hands will I carve the vitals from him!"

He might well have carried out his threat, except that Carlos fled desperately. Not until months later, when Don Miguel had dispatched two Indian trailers, was he found and brought back. But when the Indians led him once more into the home patio, Carlos displayed a leather sack.

"*Oro,* Don Miguel!" the lad cried. "*Mucho oro!* With this gold you can truly be wealthy. I found it in a mountain far to the north. There is much more!"

He opened a bag of the richest nuggets human eyes had ever beheld.

Don Miguel forgave Carlos, the lover, and hired Carlos, the explorer, to guide three expeditions to that distant mountain. The gold, they found, was indeed rich. It lay within a mile of a central peak shaped like the crown of a Mexican hat, hence was named *La Mina Sombrera,* the Hat Mine. The first two expeditions had to be small ones. When the United States acquired Arizona in 1848, though, Don Miguel organized a last party of some three hundred men, and six hundred pack animals, to bring out a fortune. The very size of that party begat carelessness. Savage Apache Indians swooped down on it, massacring all but two boys, who eventually got back to the home rancho with news of the tragedy.

The mine then lay idle for about thirty years, and became a vague legend. Meanwhile Anglo-Saxon settlers moved into the region. One day Jacob Walz, a bearded "Dutchman," lost his way in Superstition Mountain and was suffering acutely from thirst. He stumbled onto a trail that led him to a camp of three middle-aged Mexicans. They gave him water, then food, treated him kindly, revived him. But as he regained strength, he became curious.

"What in hellfire are you three camped up here for?" he demanded.

"*Por el oro, senor.* The gold."

"Gold? What gold?"

"*Si senor, mucho oro! La Mina Sombrera!*"

It was true. Two of these Mexicans were the boys who had escaped the massacre. They and a friend had come back, at long last, to re-work the bonanza. Moreover, they showed old Walz bags

39

of nuggets of incredible richness. Walz looked, and cupidity seized him.

Without warning he reached for his rifle and fired. Two of the Mexicans were down with one bullet.

"No, no! In the name of God - - - - !" The third screamed for mercy. But Walz fired again and killed him.

Walz dragged the bodies to a crevasse and piled rocks down on them — this is his own story, told later in Phoenix — then claimed the mine for his own. For years, after that, he took great bags of nuggets in to Phoenix, and would boast of his bonanza. But he wouldn't share it. Indeed, he ambushed and killed eight men, including his own nephew, who tried to follow him in! He was a feared and fearful old character on the Arizona scene.

One day, though, it came Jacob Walz's turn to die. Racked with pneumonia, he spoke his last words to a friend who had dropped in — Dick Holmes.

"You are the only man to befriend me, Holmes," he murmured. "You shall have my gold. I covered the mine with logs and rocks, then planted a cactus on the spot. Under my bed is a metal box. In it is a map, and some nuggets. They are all yours. The map is plain if you know the key. The key is a palo verde tree with a pointing arm. It is located not far from the Hat, the highest peak."

He told more, including details of his murders, and then died. In his memory there is a rock monument near the highway on the west front of Superstition Mountain, put there by The Dons. The caretaker there says the monument is photographed an average of seventy times a day by travelers.

And in the metal box that Walz gave to Dick Holmes? The map, as promised. And nuggets worth about $8,000.

A short time ago I photographed and handled some of those same nuggets. Dick Holmes had searched all the remainder of his life for the mine, but the Superstition fastnesses are many and wild. He died a thwarted man. His son, Brown Holmes, showed me the nuggets. They were walnut size, of almost solid gleaming or yellow gold, enough to quicken the pulse of any man.

Brown Holmes, too, has searched. The palo verde with the pointing arm has not been found; the ironwood logs still cover the mine entrance. Moreover, the fame of the place has grown, and thousands more have felt the lure of treasure in Superstition Mountain. Many have come searching. At least six lives are known to have been lost on the mountain within the past few years.

Most spectacular was the story of Adolf Ruth. One June he went into Superstition alone, and never returned. Two months of intense search by sheriff's posses and others failed to locate him. Then in December of that year an archaeological party found his gleaming skull — with a bullet hole in the temple. Half a mile away they found his headless torso and his camp. All his personal effects were intact, except that a map he owned had been stolen. It was a map acquired, significantly, from heirs of the old Peralta family in Mexico. To this day, though, nobody can say who killed Adolf Ruth. (I have given a more detailed story of the Lost Dutchman legend in my book *Ghost Gold*.)

Many similar episodes are on record. Meyer Schuelebtz of New York City came west to search for treasure. The inevitable happened; he became lost in the mountain, and almost died of thirst and exposure before he stumbled into a camp of prospectors. Sheriff James Herron and a posse had been searching for Schuelebtz for days — and six of the searchers were fired on by "somebody" with rifles from across a deep canyon.

Yet another gold seeker, ex-Marine Davis O'Hara of Milwaukee, went into Superstition and became lost. After circling two days, and sleeping two nights in caves where panthers had denned, he found his own camp. He stumbled to it, weak from hunger.

Lo, the camp had been raided! His tent, his personal effects, everything had been destroyed. Not stolen, but destroyed, by human hands. Whose hands? Your guess is as good as O'Hara's.

About eight thousand people a year now go into Superstition hunting the Dutchman's gold, some with tongue in cheek, but most with high if hidden hopes. Other hordes search for the hundreds of other treasures. Coronado himself led the most magnificent treasure hunt in history through a part of this region, traveling with three hundred companions and six hundred animals for five thousand or more miles. "And while they did not find riches," wrote his chronicler, Castaneda, "they found a place in which to search." They did indeed.

The very history of the region is dated from strike to strike. In 1848 one discovery in California stampeded a nation. California in turn was stampeded by subsequent strikes in Colorado, Arizona, Nevada, and Texas. Henry Wickenburg, in anger, picked up a rock to throw at a contrary pack burro, but he saw a glint of yellow as he threw. The Vulture Mine he opened there has produced $50,000,000. Ed Schieffelin in 1879 got off his mule to inspect two human skeletons lying on the desert. Between their outstretched hands lay a pile of silver nuggets. He scouted for the source, found it, and established the deathless helldorado town of Tombstone.

It is the tale of *lost* gold that lures us most, and it always rings with a tone of probability. Go talk, as I have, to elderly John Davis down in the Cheery Cows — that being local idiom for the Chiricahua Mountains.

"My parents ranched here," says he, "when there wasn't a bank in five hundred miles. They bought and sold cattle and other stuff with gold coin. They protected that coin the best way they could. Mama used to tell of burying it in glass jars under fence posts.

"One quart jar of gold held most of their life's savings, and they didn't draw on it much, or ever tell where it was hid. But Geronimo's Apaches killed Mama and Papa suddenly, one day in 1881, and not one of us six children has located that jar. I'm the only child left, and I've given up."

Posts, usually of mesquite or ironwood, don't rot easily in that dry semi-desert soil. Do you blame me for inspecting every post

42

within a dozen miles of the Davis ranch house? I helped dig out one such family cache, after a death, in which nearly $600 was concealed, but I had no claim to any of it. We know, too, that other pioneers used hollow trees, caves, thick adobe walls, even graves, as burial spots for their valuables. Wagon trains, afraid of bandits, often buried their money, then built a campfire over the spot. Indians massacred every man in one such train known to have carried about $20,000 — and I know who found that money, in 1943.

The site was near an air-training field, and one night I was drafted to give a little entertainment lecture to some of the boys. It was natural to draw on local lost-treasure lore and, as the saying is, they ate it up. Two days later, a Sunday, they had me back. They had rigged up an electric "doodlebug," a contraption with ear phones that buzzed if a big coil of wire was brought near any metal body. Would I show them the exact camp ground of the wagon train?

We milled around there all afternoon. We tried to reason out just where the wagons must have formed a circle, thence where the campfires might have been built. Four times the doodlebug buzzed, and the lads dug up iron buckets, tires, hubs, and such. That's the trouble with those scientific divining gadgets, they'll sound off for a sewer pipe as quickly as for a robbers' cache. We got nowhere. But I observed one quiet chap standing apart, watching.

Two months later, he had gone back alone. I got the details from an Indian who hauled a load of fireplace wood to my home, and who had quietly watched him. The lad had obtained a long soil auger and bored perhaps a hundred holes. Finally he struck something, for he had excavated a bigger hole, about four feet deep. At the bottom was the unmistakable shape of a small trunk, the "boot" used for shipping specie by stagecoach or wagon.

When I called at camp this boy was in the air, and when I called again he was on his way to England. I did not tell on him, but I did pump a few of his buddies. Sure enough, "something had happened" to the young man, for his friends described his great excitement, beyond what he had felt about the departure for Europe.

That's the best near miss I've had, unless we speculate on the old adobe dwelling that stood for sixty years in Phoenix at Fifth Avenue and Monroe Street. I had heard by some grapevine that stagecoach bandits had once lived there. But I was late. The floor had been partially torn up, and a hole had been dug. For drama's sake I put a friend in the hole and took a photograph, then went away trying to feel skeptical. There had been no real evidence of treasure in the hole. Two nights later a friend on the police force telephoned.

"Say," he began, "we just had a call from that Monroe Street adobe. Somebody's working in there with a flashlight. Thought you might want a tip."

We gathered there quickly, but again too late. Somebody had made a strike. There was a fresh hole, in another corner near the mud brick wall. Broken pieces of pottery jars, and a small, rotted rawhide sack, were there. We found one coin by sifting the soil, just one. We tried to keep the matter quiet, hoping, but it leaked out and fellow treasure hunters all but lifted that adobe off its foundations until its owner finally had it razed.

Frederick San Diego Rawson, who lived past ninety and who mule-wagoned from Canada to Mexico and from Denver to Los Angeles, once showed me a pocket full of nuggets, worth perhaps $2,000.

"I come to a cabin once in a snortin' blizzard," said he. "Found two burros froze to death outside. Pushed the door in and discovered an old man stiff as a post on the floor. Been dead maybe a month, and froze solid. But he'd took charcoal from his fireplace and lettered on the bottom of the door."

He sketched it for me, from memory:

GOLD HID IN BUNK — MINE IS DO - - - - -

He found the dead man's cache cleverly hidden in a false bottom of the bunk under a straw mattress. Obviously the man had known

44

he would die, and apparently did die before he finished his message. "Mine is —" where? Down- Down where? Neither Mr. Rawson nor I was ever able to determine.

C. W. McKee, another old-timer of excellent reputation, came to my home with news that he had found the Mine with the Iron Door. He may have, at that.

It was one of those storied instances in which "My uncle got this old Spanish map down in Mexico, see?" Almost invariably, such maps mark the treasure site with a Holy Cross. This one did. But this one went a step further and helped you locate the exact mountain, too, and bless me, if Mr. McKee didn't go there, probe behind some bushes, and find an old mine shaft. It wasn't far from that Tumacacori Mission, where early-day Spaniards were known to have had considerable ore.

Mr. McKee's map was found dramatically in a hollowed-out handle of a stone knife. The stone was beautifully chiseled. Other rocks found nearby had cryptic designs cut into them. Mr. McKee felt that they pointed to a cache of 2,500,000 ounces of gold which, legend said, was already mined. He failed to solve the mystery, and all of us willing followers have also failed.

That Tumacacori is a place for dreaming of the past. But what of the olla of golden nuggets "positively" buried near the garden wall?

I first tried to find them, rather casually, in 1927. But digging is work, and I ended up like many another devotee of ghost gold — dozing in the sun. I was on my honeymoon anyway, and so had other interests.

But later I went back and learned something that fired my fever for treasure all over again. Many times, around many campfires, I had "heard tell" of an Indian raid on Tumacacori in 1821. It was said that the padres themselves were killed without revealing the treasure's location. Over the years, this took stature as a folk tale and nothing else. But one day in 1920, just ninety-nine years after the raid, a devout Mexican walked up to two National Monument

45

rangers in Arizona, removed his straw hat, crossed himself, and spoke. Politely, almost apologetically, he announced that from his grandfather he had learned the location of Tumacacori's golden chalice.

They didn't believe him. But, just in case, they went to the specified spot, a few feet up the side of the ancient wall, back near the altar itself, removed two thick adobe bricks, and — there it was! The chalice is safe now with the padres at San Xavier Mission, near Tucson.

From that moment the government has directed all search at Tumacacori, but the rest of us like to peck at the nearby hills. I have a fine old Spanish stirrup which may have been Coronado's own, that came from the rocks near there. I have seen old coins, long-roweled spurs, bayonets and swords found nearby. But no one has found the main treasure cache.

I have heard that the olla of nuggets is not hidden in the mission proper, but in the ancient graveyard. But ghouling does not appeal to me, even if I might dodge the rangers.

Near the town of Pantano, in Pima County, Arizona, three robbers one day dropped off the Southern Pacific train as it pulled from the station. They made their way to the baggage room, all entering it at about the same time.

"Don't make no sudden movement!" a hard voice commanded the express agent. "Now, hands up toward the roof." Black pistols and black masks made the command an emphatic one.

While the trainman pointed obligingly to the ceiling, the robbers collected sixteen Wells Fargo express bags, containing a total of $40,000. Then they tied the hapless agent, took their loot and fled. Fresh horses, saddled and ready, had been stationed nearby.

It was only a few hours later that the Pima county sheriff, Bob Leatherwood, was on their trail with a heavy posse, and he saw that the trail was fresh. Leatherwood promptly deduced that his quarry had headed for the Rincon Mountains and most likely for Colossal Cave. He led his men in a short cut and pulled up presently at a ranch cabin. Back of the corral were the lathery mounts of the robbers, still panting from their run. But the bandits themselves were on their way again, with fresh horses.

The possemen easily picked up the trail again, and it led straight to the cave's entrance. As they galloped up to it a devastating volley of gunfire met the men of the law. Two of them fell, and others were wounded.

A quick run to the shelter of rocks saved further immediate loss, and in a few seconds the mouth of the cave was under heavy siege. But no direct targets inside the yawning mouth of the cavern could be found. So the sheriff prepared to starve out the bandits.

Camp was made, and all night long a vigil was kept. But not another shot came from the robbers.

The silent siege continued throughout the next day and night, and the next and the next. Sheriff Leatherwood figured that he could starve the men into surrender cheaper than he could overpower them in battle. One morning he crawled as close as he dared, well within calling distance of the cave, and yelled to the bandits.

"You men will save time if you come out now," he shouted. "We are going to starve you out. Come out with your hands up and nobody will be hurt."

He listened but heard no answer. The sheriff backed off, to carry on his siege. Two or three men could guard that cave entrance forever, with only three bandits inside.

But that afternoon a cowboy rode within sight, and when hailed by the possemen, heard their story with astonishment.

"Why, you men are barking down the wrong hole, Sheriff!" he told Leatherwood. "Them bandits was seen yesterday over at Willcox!"

Pressed for details, the cowboy described the three men thought to be in the cavern, exactly as had the expressman who was robbed.

Sheriff Leatherwood picked up his rifle and walked to the cave entrance. His posse followed him, but not a sign of the robbers could be found.

47

The men then built fires on a number of spots as far inside the cave as they could conveniently penetrate, and stationed other men over a big area outside to watch.

Sure enough, in a few minutes a thread of smoke curled up from some bushes on the opposite side of the mountain, coming through a well-like crevice about forty feet deep. It was just big enough to permit a man to crawl through, but it was the avenue through which the bandits had escaped.

A few months later the bandits again ran afoul of a sheriff's posse in northern Arizona, far from the cave. Two of them were killed in this battle, and the third taken to jail. He subsequently was sent to the penitentiary. The money was not recovered.

He stayed in prison twenty-eight years, and all that time he repeatedly swore that he knew nothing of where the $40,000 was hidden. He insisted that the three bandits had split their loot and buried it in three separate places, unknown to each other. When he was released, a Wells Fargo express agent was put on his trail again, shadowing him. But the man was shrewd. He guessed that he would so be watched, and he played safe for two more years. Then he suddenly moved fast. The detective lost him, but went to the cave and investigated. A hole had been dug inside and beside it were leather coin bags — empty! The bandit had claimed his third of the loot, and has not been heard of.

Today you can go there and try to find the other two thirds. But don't be too hopeful. Colossal Cave has a known thirty-nine miles of hallways, great cathedral-like rooms, ghostly formations of limestone, secret nooks and dens. Aladdin would have been quite at home, which is more than I am when I poke into the cavern. If you are imaginative enough to be a lost-treasure hunter in the first place, the eerie atmosphere in the Bandit's Den will all but embalm you. If you regard it simply as a "point of interest" it is still eminently worth your visiting.

The physical obstacles in treasure hunting are often terrific. In a creek bed in Walnut Canyon, Arizona, lies an iron safe with a mine payroll and much gold dust, reputedly untouched for over half a century. A flood broke a dam upstream, sending water, trees and rocks roaring down onto a tiny village. Houses were demolished, people killed, the safe buried somewhere under fifty yards of dirt and debris. You'd think that a thing as big as a safe could have been re-located, but just one horseback ride down the canyon impresses you anew with the overwhelming power of nature. One glimpse at what a flood can do is enough to shrivel any man's ego.

It takes, then, a certain courage, a boundless physical energy, and a deathless optimism, to remain a professional hunter of hidden treasure. Better fun, at least for one of my somewhat sedentary inclinations, is to specialize in the legends, the histories, the yarns, all those more romantic aspects of the matter.

That academic approach will still force you outdoors, perhaps all you can stand. You must go into the back country by high-axle car, on horses, on burros at times, and certainly on foot. You must learn that water stored in a bisnaga cactus can be sheer nectar when you are half insane with thirst, and that mule meat cooked by the sun is nourishing. You must learn to squat in camp, hang your arms over your knees, smoke slowly, and stare off into space while your newest specimen — some wrinkled old mystic of the hills — gives you a new conception of time. It is from him that you will hear details of the Mother Lode, whence come all pure gold findings. He will know within a mile where to find the Lost Virgin Mine, the Nigger Ben, the San Saba, the Lost Pegleg which grows and grows in value as the years pass, the *Planchas de Plata* (planks of silver), the Lost Sixshooter, and the Phantom Stage.

From a distillation of what his kind tells, you will learn four ways to start your search for treasure or to become an important character in a treasure legend. They are:

1. Get lost on the desert, preferably in a sandstorm. Lose your burro and pack outfit, canteen, and gun. Stagger eventually into some isolated trading post. Of course you will have picked up

priceless nuggets somewhere en route. But you can never quite find the spot again.

2. Befriend an Indian. Find one with a broken leg, doctor him, and lug him to his wickiup. Sure as fate he will eventually come to repay the kindness and, lacking money, will lead you blind-folded to an amazingly rich outcropping of virgin gold. Take a good bagful of it while you can, for you won't come back. Indians don't talk much, and you can't remember how you traveled, eyes covered. Sucker that I am, I have tried valiantly to backtrack men so favored. I am still poor.

3. Find an old map in your grandfather's trunk. It must be wrinkled, faded, cryptic, but legible. It helps if it is drawn on home-made parchment or on any smooth, tanned animal skin. Such maps are real, for our regional libraries have some of them, and I have seen at least a dozen. When they tie in, even in part, with existing word-of-mouth lore about the treasure Grandpappy had, they are inflaming.

4. Go into Mexico, act natural, ask questions. But don't let down your guard. For two centuries professional storytellers have roamed the back country of Sonora and Baja California, entertaining villagers for small fees. These talented performers have built up a terrific legend of lost treasure, and over the years much of the legend has gradually acquired the dignity of fact, at least in people's minds. Unscrupulous ones now will sell you those facts for whatever fee you will pay, and throw in a map so genuine in appearance that your credulity will swell. One such genius, a picture-book character named Jesus Maria Gilberto del Munoz de la Velarde y Hernandez, is memorable, for he stumbled onto a true treasure story. Recently I asked him why he told about the treasure for years, yet did not search.

"Finally I did go, *amigo*," he confessed. "But one man I had told, he had already gone." He flung back his *serape* to spread his hands in a gesture of utter dejection.

I knew just how he felt. Frustration is a common penalty for us who too-cynically ride the ghost gold trail.

## VI.  THE BIG BOLD BARON

The fascinating lore of Arizona does indeed center much around its flora and fauna, and assuredly around its hidden treasure as we have just seen. But there's one other category which lends us glamor; one notorious character who is essential to truly good wild-western drama on any stage. He is of course the villain, the Bad Man. Good men are nice and we all classify ourselves among them, but nobody talks or reads about us very much, whereas one scowling outlaw — wearing a black hat and riding a black horse (good men ride white horses) — will rivet everybody's rapt attention.

I could here and now parade a whole troop of such Bad Men before you, for Arizona has spawned a shameful number of them, indeed I have already referred to a few. But let me now brag: Arizona developed the *baddest* Bad Man America ever knew! Some knowledge of his exploits is a must if you would be indoctrinated with regional lore, and assuredly he can be a fine representative of all the blackguards who ever roamed these wild western hills.

His name was James Reavis.

Jim set a high for rascality which is almost incredible. He became the most artistic — but wait! Let's allow his true story to

53

unfold in natural, chronological sequence, remembering always that it is taken directly from the records of the United States courts.

Jim's adult career began during the Civil War, when he discovered that he could obtain delightfully long furloughs from fighting by the simple expedient of forging an order for leave of absence. For this, he never was caught. After the war, Jim gained minor business success by driving a mule which pulled a streetcar in St. Joseph, Missouri. The mule was slow, patronage was small. Jim, still young, had ample time to daydream as he rolled along.

In view of what subsequently happened, we must assume that he often said to himself something like this:

"Wouldn't it be great to get away from this and go west to make my fortune! I'd like to be one of these Spanish noblemen I read about. Have a lot of land, and a big hacienda, and servants and horses and herds of cattle and all that. Then all the people would bow to me. I could ride in a high-wheeled carriage, with fast horses stepping high. And wear a big sombrero braided in gold. And a red serape, and velvet jacket and pants. I could eat fine food, and travel with a pretty woman wherever I wanted to go. Maybe somewhere down in the southwest where the Spanish caballeros live. Where people serenade and play guitars and dance . . . . ."

Jim Reavis must have dreamed dreams like that often.

And his daydreams must have been stimulated by the literature of the day. Spaniards had settled in New Mexico, and in Arizona, Texas, and California. They had brought a beautiful heritage of color and romance, a love of beauty and fine living. There had been a war with Mexico. There was a continuous westward movement of Americans to settle in the lands in which the Spaniards had previously settled. Such dreams as Reavis had were not fantastic at all — as dreams. They must have whiled away many a weary afternoon, while Jim pecked with his whip at the rump of a lazy streetcar mule.

One day Jim Reavis disappeared from public life in Missouri. About five years later, citizens down in the still wild Arizona

54

and New Mexico Territories were served with a formally worded and official-looking manifesto.

The announcement said, in effect, that persons now situated on "la Baronia de Arizonac," otherwise known as the Barony of Arizona, would henceforth be required to pay the necessary feudal fees, or to relinquish possession of property and remove themselves therefrom.

The manifesto was not especially threatening. Just formal, and definite. For the benefit of any persons not well informed, it was explained that title to the barony was held by virtue of an old Spanish grant, not unlike several others resulting from the days of Spanish occupation, and all held legal by the Government of the United States.

Finally — and with delightful nonchalance — the boundaries of the barony itself were given.

They were casually said to include an area extending from a point west of Phoenix, Arizona, away over into the present State of New Mexico!

The dimensions were seventy-five miles north and south by two hundred and twenty-five miles east and west — some twelve million acres.

The vast barony included the present Salt River Valley, irrigated by the Roosevelt Dam, and the Casa Grande Valley, irrigated now by the Coolidge Dam. Even then the valleys were partly under irrigation and had attracted a high type of farmers. The irrigable Salt River Valley alone totaled some four hundred thousand acres.

The value of the barony, estimated at a minimum, was ten dollars per acre, or a total of one hundred and twenty million dollars!

Every town of importance then in Arizona, except Tucson, was included in the barony. The great copper, silver, and gold mines around Globe, Miami, Superior, and Ray were included. All mineral rights, water rights, grazing rights, and any other assets of the land were automatically the property of the present owner of the barony, the manifesto explained.

55

Finally, it explained that the present owner was one Don James Addison de Peralta-Reavis, Baron of Arizona, the legal heir of the first Baron of Arizona, who had received the property direct from the King of Spain more than a century before.

All of these pronouncements were more than a bit stunning to the citizens of Arizona and New Mexico, and considerable talk naturally ensued. But this was as nothing compared to the furore created when His Excellency Baron James and the Baroness Sofia Loreto rode one day into their barony.

"There was a carriage with the highest wheels I ever saw," one contemporary has recorded. "It was black and shiny as water. A coat of arms was painted on the doors in gold. It was pulled by six horses, all solid white, with red and gold trappings.

"When a man got out, we knew he was important. He was about six feet tall, maybe half an inch less. He was lean, but proud-looking. He wore a big gray hat with a high crown and it had gold all over it. He had on black pants with red lacings clean down the sides, and a purple coat or jacket. He wore two pistols and a red shawl hung over his shoulder."

The people knew instantly, of course, that he was a rich Spaniard. He had the manner as well as the clothes, even though his face lacked the characteristic Latin swarthiness and features. His conduct was rather magnificent, on the whole. He didn't behead anybody, or issue any dictatorial orders, as a storybook baron might have done. More or less unconsciously, the yokels and others of the isolated region removed their hats, and called him "Sir" and "Don James." He was completely gracious with all, assuring them that he hoped for nothing but happiness on the part of his settlers, and that he had large plans for developing the barony.

With just the proper flourishes, he presented to Dona Sofia, also attired in Spanish finery, those who seemed to merit such an introduction. She smiled graciously, explained occasionally that, although the baronial estate was really hers by right of inheritance,

56

she of course had turned full ownership and administration of it over to her beloved husband Don James, as became a woman.

Don James usually did nothing so crass as discuss business matters with the settlers. He just "inspected" the barony. Hired agents attended to the commercial details — such petty matters as collecting a thousand dollars from one farmer, five hundred dollars from another, two thousand dollars from the next.

In due time, Don James did confer with distinguished men, either in Arizona or in the big cities, when he needed their services. These men included Robert G. Ingersoll, Charles Crocker, Roscoe Conkling, and Collis P. Huntington — men whose names dominated any Who's Who of that era. They and others of distinction were glad to greet Don James as a social equal and financial superior. If any of them suspected that the baron had once prodded a sleepy streetcar mule, it didn't matter; he had since married a pretty Spanish woman of extreme wealth, and he wasn't the first man to marry riches.

Moreover, during formal business routine and because of personal interest, these and other men, including agents for the United States Government, had repeatedly inspected the baron's credentials, the papers by which he claimed the extensive domain. Don James invited all and sundry to write to Mexico City — or even to Madrid, Spain — to trace the barony to the king who had granted it. When this was done, everything was found in perfect order. Musty old documents testified in minute detail to his ownership. Don James had simply, it seemed certain, married a girl who had inherited the famed Peralta Grant, which by treaty the United States was obligated to hold intact for its heirs. Come in, Don James — have the softest seat and a couple of the best cigars!

The papers concerning the inheritance approached one hundred thousand words in length, more than most modern novels. They were phrased in picturesque Spanish language. They traced ancestries, gifts, and grants, describing the person who formerly held the barony.

The first baron especially must have been great, with a truly marvelous ancestry. Sworn and signed documents indicated that this

57

gentleman of eighteenth-century Spain, one Don Miguel, was "Baron de Arizonac and Caballero de los Colorados, Gentleman of the King's Chamber with privilege to enter at will, Grandee of Spain, Knight of the Military Order of the Golden Fleece and of the Montesa, Knight of the Royal Order of Carlos III, Knight of the Insignia of the Royal College of Our Lady of Guadalupe." It was also indicated that he was "the legitimate son of Don Jose Gaston Gomez de Silva y Montez de Oca de la Cerda y de Carillo de Peralta de las Falces de la Vega (his father), and of Dona Francisca Maria Garcia de la Cordoba y Muniz de Perez (his mother), who married in the year one thousand and six hundred and eighty-six!"

Both the great and the humble of America were impressed, because Don James seemed unquestionably genuine. The Southern Pacific Railroad paid him fifty thousand dollars for a right of way across his barony. The Silver King Mine and others paid similar sums for limited mineral rights. Clearances of title were sold by the hundreds to lesser men — farmers, ranchers, and such. If any man complained, other citizens shamed him for his presumption.

Jim Reavis — Don James Addison de Peralta-Reavis — was literally sitting on top of the financial and social world. He maintained mansions in Madrid, Washington, St. Louis, and London, and admittedly spent about sixty thousand dollars a year on travel alone. His position, backed by the elaborately complete documents, seemed impregnable.

One day, however, Tom Weedin, an Arizona printer, was examining some of the Peralta Grant papers. A hobby of Tom's was the study of history, and he loved to browse in old court files. And being a good printer, he knew much about type faces, paper and ink. Consequently, something he unexpectedly noticed while looking at the Peralta Grant papers set his heart pounding.

"I'll be durned!" he said. "This old paper about the baron's grant — it has some printing from a type that wasn't invented till 1875. But the paper is dated 1748!"

And in another place was a reference to certain colonies in

New Spain, on a paper dated two years before the colonies had even been established!

The papers were obviously "authentic." The ink was faded, the handwriting and language foreign, the signatures and seals duly attested. Every authority had said so.

Tom Weedin was sorely confused. He browsed further.

On another document, from the archives at Madrid and dated 1787, he found a faint watermark from a Wisconsin paper mill established about 1870.

Forthwith Tom hastened to federal officers to report his find.

With skilled help, the government agents discovered other discrepancies. The Spanish words *por* and *para* (both meaning "for" in English, but each with definite shades of meaning) were erroneously interchanged in some of the Peralta Grant papers. Other mistakes of this kind were found — idiomatic errors which no genuine Spaniard, especially a well-educated government clerk or priest of that time (such as would have written the documents) would ever have made.

Before long, news of the suspected swindle began to leak out, and Don James himself was confronted with the evidence. He tried persistent bluffing. He invited more investigation, claiming that somebody was trying by forgery to persecute him. He ostentatiously demanded a court hearing of his land claims.

That's precisely what he got.

He had bluffed Uncle Sam for six years or so, but the federal agents were now determined on a showdown. The Court of Private Land Claims had just been created (amid great political turmoil), and the Peralta-Reavis case was exactly in its jurisdiction.

The detailed court records of that hearing read like a moving picture scenario, because into them went — after great effort — the full story of Jim Reavis's career. Later he issued his own confession.

"His confession was so astounding," said one government agent at the time, "that it would be put down as the craziest of fiction, except for the fact that our investigations proved it true in almost every detail.

59

"It is obvious that Reavis succeeded through the sheer bigness of his claim. A lesser swindle, attempted by a less imaginative man, would have aroused suspicion earlier. But Reavis possessed infinite patience, and a passion for detail. He took five years to perfect his groundwork. When he finally stepped out in his gay Spanish clothing and with his Spanish wife, his foundation as the baron was practically perfect."

Reavis saw a chance to make his daydreams as a Spanish don come true when a Missouri real estate agent showed him a paper in a faked land sale in the southwest. It referred to a small and spurious "Peralta Grant," but the document itself was rather imposing. Reavis figured he might make a big thing of it. And bless Pat, he did!

He got hold of the paper and went to San Francisco. He landed a job as wandering reporter for a newspaper. Then he began a systematic stuffing of government records in Mexico City, in Seville, and in Madrid, and on the side he built up a perfectly delightful personal romance. The young man unquestionably had a way with him.

The girl, Dona Sofia Loreto, he often referred to as his "Andalusian beauty." The only known photograph of her shows her to be rather plump, but pretty nevertheless. "Her features incline to the Jewish type," Reavis himself wrote. "Her eyes are large, and of darkest hazel. She has a profusion of black silken hair." Her exquisite grace and fascination helped prove her to be of noble ancestry.

But she wasn't of noble ancestry.

She had been a foundling, a waif, raised in servitude by a California family. Because she was half-Indian, she had a dark skin. Reavis discovered her by accident, took her (but never actually married her, he said), educated her patiently and thoroughly into the belief that she really was the lawful heir of the great (but fictitious) first Baron of Arizona, Don Miguel etcetera.

Reavis found people who remembered when the girl had been born. He dug up a historic incident of the same year, skillfully connected the birth with it, and had a noble Spanish family coming through California and stopping there for the girl's birth. The court records from Reavis's trial in Santa Fe, New Mexico, reveal even such intimate details as the birth pangs suffered when Reavis's spurious Spanish wife was born. And witnesses, hired by Reavis and misled by him, actually testified to every claim he made in the matter.

With this pre-empted half-Indian waif, Reavis from Missouri set out to build his heritage. He took her to Spain with him.

"Browsing in curio shops there," he confessed, "I found beautiful little miniature paintings of a man and a woman of noble mien. I learned that the family had long ago died out. I bought the miniatures, convinced my wife they were her great-grandparents, the first baron and baroness."

This worked so well, Reavis found, that he went even further. Before he was through, he had a full-size family of ancestors for the girl, with beautiful paintings of them all. Those paintings, too, were introduced in the trial in the Court of Private Land Claims at Santa Fe.

No less cleverly or carefully worked out was Reavis's confessed method of stuffing the official records.

It was easy, he discovered, to hire a disinterested letter writer or scribe, such as every Spanish or Mexican town still has, to translate or copy, for a small fee, any given document as directed. Reavis would gain admittance to the real records, posing as a newspaperman (which in truth he was after a fashion). He would note the exact form of the pages in the musty, dusty old records, the type of writing, the margins, the ink — every detail. Some were written, some were partly printed. He could buy printing cheaply, too. Whatever was necessary, he would prepare — documents substituting his own fictitious family names and describing the gift of La Baronia de Arizonac to the first baron in the minutest detail, giving landmarks, survey lines, boundaries, and even maps.

But how did he get those forged documents into the actual old records?

That was easy, too, for a resourceful man. Reavis told exactly how in his confession.

"I went into one place as a newspaper writer and obtained permission to see the archives," he said. "A priest was very anxious to serve me, to help all he could, as I appeared interested, respectful. But I didn't want him hanging around in sight all the time. He stayed and stayed.

"Finally, I fell over in a pretended faint.

"The priest let out a cry, and ran away to summon aid for me. Quickly I jumped up, slipped some pages out of the archives at the right place, and inserted my own, which looked just like them but read differently. No one saw me.

"Then I lay back down, concealing the removed papers in my clothing. The priest came with another priest carrying some fine wine. I drank it and 'revived' easily. Then I thanked them and went away."

Five years of this sort of careful build-up were enough to make his claims foolproof, Jim Reavis felt. He had found it easy to convince his own woman and the Spanish authorities to whom he talked. It ought to be easy, he thought, to convince the residents of Arizona and New Mexico.

And he was correct. When he showed up in the American Southwest, he was accepted for what he purported to be — a wealthy grandee, backed by a heritage from the King of Spain. Quickly Jim Reavis turned his imaginary wealth into real riches, by collecting fees from men who used his baronial lands.

The pomp and display with which he had lived became well known. He traveled and entertained extensively. He donated a thousand dollars for an altar cloth at a Guadalajara cathedral. To the people in Monterrey he gave a drinking fountain at a cost of fifteen hundred dollars. He showered gifts wherever he or his wife was in a mood to do so. With their twin sons, who were dressed in regal finery, they traveled to the swankiest places in Europe and America. The United States Ambassador in Madrid entertained him lavishly. Everywhere the baron and baroness were accorded respect, until the spurious structure was deflated and Don James Addison de Peralta-Reavis — now plain Jim Reavis again — was standing before a federal judge to be sentenced.

And what punishment was meted? For the biggest swindler in American history?

Two years.

# VII.   VANISHED EMPIRE

Citizens in every land have always been interested in and usually proud of their history. This holds for Arizona, though our history is short. But we have a *pre*-history which stimulates more than pride; it is downright exciting. Our Hohokam (pronounced ho-ho-KAHM), an Indian word meaning People Who Were Here Before, accomplished things that tax our credulity; here in the sun country scientists have laid bare remains of an ancient civilization startling in their significance. No one can truly appreciate this region without some knowledge of those ancients, nor fail to be impressed by them once he has projected his thinking back into their time.

There were two main groups of them; storybook folk, yet very real, who left us a priceless heritage, setting highest possible standards in what we call creativity and adaptability. Study them with respect, starting with —

## 1. The Valley People

On the cactus-guarded desert of southern Arizona, prehistoric folk moved millions of cubic yards of earth and dug some 230 miles of main-trunk canals to divert water from the Salt and Gila rivers. Without beasts of burden, with the crudest implements imaginable, these ancient canal builders also constructed cities which had flourished, declined, and been forgotten before Columbus sailed.

They left no parchments, scrolls or tablets for our discovery. But the very land is steeped with their lore; from the ruins of their cities students have determined an unexpected multitude of details to prove the fullness of their cultures. Thousands of cubic yards of earth have been painstakingly removed from the ruins of their homes. Books have been written and countless reports have been entered into institutional records. Those prehistoric folk are known to us better than are some of our nineteenth-century white pioneers.

In an area embracing the better part of the Salt and Gila valleys, those ancients built their empires. Exactly where they came from is not known. Evidence suggests that migrations were made from Asia to Alaska thence southward into our semi-tropical climate. Over unknown centuries those folk married and lived and worked and fought and fused, evolving that culture whose remains we see today.

Some tremendous necessity drove them into reclaiming their vast desert area. It is almost as large as that which modern white man, with all his fine machinery and engineering methods, has recently reclaimed. To irrigate the Salt River Valley in the current century man has had to spend millions of dollars in federal money, has built Roosevelt and other great storage dams, has used thousands of horses, mules, trucks, cranes and steam shovels, has used electricity, iron, steel, copper and cement. The ancients used just two things to do a similar job — man power, and little flat pieces of stone!

From the remains of their irrigation systems, numerous maps have been drawn tracing the old canals. It is marvelous to observe how they held to the topography of the land. Their only surveying "instrument" was some old brown-skinned gentleman in breechclout squatting and squinting into the sun. Yet they worked with precision, so expertly following the slope for water flow that modern surveyors have been able to follow the old remains for miles and miles. They built brush-and-rock dams across a river half a mile wide, solely by hand. They diverted water into canals fifty feet wide at the bottom and seventy-five at the top, and twelve feet deep. They knew how to grade those canals so the water would flow, yet gently enough not to tear away the bank.

Scientists today are walking along those ancient ditches kicking up dirt and digging down a few feet to find countless stone hoes. Literally thousands of them may now be seen in collections all over the state. With these "flat rocks" each the size of your two spread hands or smaller, the laborers hacked and scraped then scooped the dirt into baskets to be carried away. Similar methods were used in building clan houses and fortresses, protective walls and homes.

A casual showplace for tourists today is Casa Grande, called America's first skyscraper. It is a four-story structure, still standing forty feet high, made of native mud and plaster. It is among the most recent of such buildings, for it was abandoned less than a thousand years ago. Authorities think that the last few lingering tribes of dark-skinned farmers, starved out by drouth and bedeviled by nomadic enemies, finally left the building and city just a few years before Columbus started to the New World. The skyscraper is located in the Gila Valley of Arizona near the modern town of Coolidge. Its name, Casa Grande, is Spanish simply for "Big House."

Almost inconceivable labor went into its construction. Its walls are six feet thick at the bottom and were made of a peculiar mixture something like concrete, based on the native *caliche* soil. Similar construction went into walls of the amphitheater, the storage rooms, the dwellings and the defense parapets that make up the compound about the central tower. Erection of the tower itself required hundreds of baskets of mud to raise the wall one foot, and there are literally miles of other walls.

Significant, too, is the wood used in that construction work at Casa Grande, as in the fifty-odd other prehistoric ruins of towns and cities scattered about this vanished realm. Vast quantities of wood were used in Casa Grande's construction, wood of a type that

67

could not have grown nearer than eighty miles away. Even the heavy rafters were cut and brought out of the distant mountains, again with crude stone tools and man's own labor, in an era long before Spanish introduction of horses and mules.

The entire compound of Casa Grande was surrounded by a defense wall, 216 by 420 feet. Nearby were similar compounds, some larger, some smaller. The inhabitants had little space in living quarters; an average room was barely five by seven feet and not quite high enough for a tall man to stand. Two rooms probably housed most families.

Frequently the dwelling rooms had no doors or windows. The houses were entered through holes in the roofs, by means of ladders on the outside which could be pulled up for safety. Inside was the combined living-dining-bedroom, which in addition was frequently the workshop, the dog kennel, and sometimes the family cemetery. Bodies of the dead might be deposited in the hollowed-out floor, a few inches below the living; or might be buried in a room wall, puddled with fresh mud and completely sealed over with fresh plaster. Both types of burials have been found, and numerous crematory ollas and pots have been unearthed.

At some ruins almost every trowelful of earth discloses such treasures as pottery and artifacts of all sorts, records of an ancient race. In all excavation work of this kind, extreme care must be practiced, for one careless move of a shovel or pick might destroy something of great value. Wherever possibility of findings is suspected, the archaeologist and his helpers use tiny whisk brooms, teaspoons, even fine paint brushes, to remove the earth. Thus no enlightening bit of decayed bone, no age-old cup or piece of ceremonial jewelry is disturbed or lost until the observer has had at least a momentary study. Infinite patience of course is required.

But the explorers of the mounds in this area have not always been archaeologists, or patient. At La Ciudad ruin in Phoenix, which was just a drab mound of earth used for coasting on bicycles when first opened, hundreds of pieces of pottery were stolen by vandals.

They used picks and shovels and destroyed more treasures than they took away. One real estate man leveled a canal builder's home and on the spot built a modern subdivision. One modern Arizona farmer collected relics from an ancient mound on his property and sold them to pay his taxes. Another used, for a hayrack, walls that were standing when Genghis Khan came roaring across Asia to conquer Europe. Still another used the foundation of an ancient clan house for the foundation of his modern cow barn. He picked up, nearby, a woman's hand mill or metate (may-TAH-tay) that was old before the Spaniards first came to this region.

Not long ago highway engineers cut through the edge of a mound "just to see what was in it." They soon quit in disgust. But a noted archaeologist reported that they had destroyed priceless information. A cotton picker built his shack on top of one valuable mound and "threw away" a lot of skulls, pots, and shards he found.

Fortunately, scientists also have received considerable help in their work. Wealthy philanthropists and foundations have aided their research, and the United States Government has declared several old villages national monuments. The City of Phoenix itself owns ancient mounds of great interest, notably Pueblo Grande four miles or so east of the downtown area and just south of Washington Street. It is a fascinating place for all visitors, because much of it has been excavated and a fine museum with continuing recorded lectures is open without charge; for Valley of the Sun folk it is the most convenient place to study those astounding ancients, the Hohokam.

Arizonans do not welcome unauthorized out-of-state "expeditions" desiring to study our mounds and other ruins. Some explorations have resulted in plain thievery, with valuable relics and other property taken to other parts of the nation without permission. But any honorable visitor is welcomed.

Long hundreds of years ago, communities had sprung up by the hundreds over the fertile southwestern desert area onto which brown folk had diverted irrigation water. Thousands of dwellings had been erected, centered about numerous clan houses or central

69

buildings which were used for religious and social centers as well as for defense. Artisans were decorating kitchen utensils and making all manner of things for personal adornment. Bone and shells they carved with masterful precision. Through tiny beads they drilled holes so small as to defy a modern needle. Domestic cotton they made into cloth, and dyed to their choice of brilliant color. At every turn in the now replete museum at Casa Grande, you may find objects to pique your interest and stimulate further study. This holds for the professional archaeologist as well as the tourist amateur or the grade school student.

At some ruins, and especially at Casa Grande, the state of preservation and the great number of artifacts have enabled students to reconstruct the daily lives of the ancient ones. The people here, it is agreed, must have been of medium stature, they were not a race of dwarfs as you might conclude when visiting the ruins and stooping to go through their doors just three or four feet high. That low doorway was a protective measure; when the house was attacked, a foe would be forced to stoop when he entered a room. Thus even one unaided woman inside could bash him over the head with a club and kill him. In such manner she would defend her home, her babies, her elderly ones, her stored corn, her jewelry, her implements, anything else she possessed, while her menfolk were outside fighting.

The inhabitants at Casa Grande had a calendar of high accuracy. Through the outer wall of the main building and through the wall of the inner room are small holes, so placed in line that on every March 7 and October 7 at sunrise the sun's rays stream through both holes to the inner room. We can imagine that these were dates of agricultural significance in the long desert growing season.

There were community ovens, and many individual rooms are still smoke stained, and piles of ashes about the corners of the rooms indicate that father and little brother objected then to carrying them out, no less than do the men of a twentieth-century family.

The frequency with which the frog motif is found in carvings and crude sculpture and various decorations suggests that those

70

people may have worshipped the frog as a rain god, much as modern Hopis think of rattlesnakes as little messengers of the gods. Perhaps the assumption was that, inasmuch as the frog appeared plentifully whenever it rained, he brought the rain with him, and since water was a major consideration of life in any desert empire, the frog was honored.

No evidence whatsoever that the southwest Hohokam employed beasts of burden has been found, but dogs they had. Dogs were buried with the younger children, probably to guide the youthful spirits over the trail to their eternal abiding place; skeletons of both together have been exhumed and studied.

Those prehistoric folk made a great variety of pottery. Vast numbers of jugs, bowls, urns, ollas, pitchers, and other vessels have been uncovered. Perhaps the biggest single piece unearthed to date is a shoulder-high olla found at the ruin known as Pueblo Primero. Three men hand-to-hand could not reach around it and it would have held many bushels of maize; we can envision the big fire and the careful tending necessary to produce it. Thousands of smaller pieces have been collected, yet one more, one funeral urn or other of rare type, can still excite our archaeologists and delight us who visit with an eye for beauty.

Pictographs or ideographs have been found in abundance on rocks near the desert cities, but usually these are attributed to later inhabitants. We have no dependable information concerning them. Eventual interpretation of the pictographs may reveal much that we want and need to know. One significant fact is that there is a definite linkage between these drawings (chiseled on rocks) and others similarly made in South America, Europe, and Asia. Consider also the maze still plainly visible on an inner wall at Casa Grande, an intricate design obviously fingered on by some ancient man when the plaster was wet; it is a duplicate of the design found on a much more ancient coin from Crete. And a bone carving found at Casa Grande, dating back a few hundred years, is a perfect Masonic Square and Compass, and Masonry dates back far indeed. Truly our prehistoric world citizens got around — or at least we can imagine they did. "Coincidence" is inadequate explanation.

At Casa Grande as at dozens of other now ruined cities, the easily defended communal buildings indicate that endless strife existed between these sedentary farmers and the nomadic hunters who resided to their north. Arizona's famed Apache Trail was first beaten out by the hoofs of horses ridden by Apache Indians swooping down to attack our Valley Pimas and Maricopas. Doubtless the ancient farmers faced similar peril, probably over that same trail.

But students agree that soil exhaustion, prolonged drouth and possibly plagues of insects were other factors in the ultimate downfall of the Hohokam. Those canal builders had no adequate storage reservoirs such as we moderns enjoy. Lacking emergency protection, then, the ancients probably went on a "hard times" basis for a few years, scrimping along on wild mesquite beans, saguaro cactus fruit, rabbit meat and such. It is not difficult to imagine families and clans gradually breaking away in search of greener pastures.

In time, then, the populations were so dwindled that defense was impossible, and so in a final series of raids the nomads may have driven out or killed the townsmen and finished their job by burning or knocking down the homes. Charred stubs of rafters and wooden supports found in the ruins are evidence of such destruction.

Generations later, other tribes doubtless settled in the valleys. Some surely made haphazard efforts at establishing permanent homes, but no race achieved even an approximation of the canal builders' success until well after the twentieth century had dawned.

## 2. High Up The Cliffs

But while the valley dwellers accomplished miracles in irrigation, home and city construction, and especially in that priceless field of human relations — getting along with one another, building happy lives — yet another group of probably the same racial stock was working out an even more improbable civilization, surely in an even more incredible environment.

This second group climbed, from necessity and/or choice, up the sheer rock walls of our canyons, found niches up there and said to one another, "This would be a good place to live." Wherefore we have the most picturesque homes and villages mankind has ever evolved.

You cannot find the cliff dwellers now; they left their cliffs centuries ago, and where they went, or why, we cannot say. Yet you may still enter their front doors, you may stare at their tools and utensils, at bits of their food and clothing, and even at mummified remains of their bodies.

For your first visit to the cliff dwellings, I would suggest Montezuma's Castle. It is sixty-five miles east of Prescott, Arizona, on a road of spectacularly beautiful scenery — deep wooded canyons, roaring streams whose waters shock your testing toe or finger, huge boulders splashed with crimson, blue and gold. As you might imagine, color motion pictures are filmed here, even though the fictional setting often is Texas or California (which have no comparable scenery). The Castle itself is in an inspired setting. Wild flowers and sycamore trees abound, and along your sinuous approach is a rivulet that mirrors all the turquoise sky. You will not see the Castle until you are virtually at its base, so concerned with camouflage were the ancients.

Whichever cliff dwelling you visit, you must come prepared for sweat and danger. Often this means climbing as high as a ten or twenty story building, not calmly on inside stairs but up the face of the slippery cliff itself, scratching for toe holds, clinging as an animal clings, and looking down on massive boulders or the tops of trees. You wonder how children and elderly folk ever managed this dizzying climb. But the cliff was protection against enemies swarming in to pillage, rape and kill. From their high ledges the cliff dwellers could drop stones down onto those enemies.

Montezuma's Castle is recommended for a first look because

73

there you do *not* have to climb. Park Rangers used to escort all visitors up the steep walls, but danger became too great, and too many thoughtless guests were desecrating the ancient homes, so that now you must look from the valley floor. But this itself is immensely rewarding; you'll scarcely believe what you see!

High up that limestone wall in a great "mouth" eroded out by winds and rains, is a clan house five stories tall and seventy feet wide, with twenty rooms. There is a narrow front porch with no railing, which makes modern mothers gasp at the thought of trying to rear children up there. But do envision some keen-eyed sentinel stationed on that porch watching, watching, staring at and studying everything that moved toward the cliff. He'd quickly spot enemies on the horizon, turn to his tom-toms and beat out a warning call to arms. Imagine the scurrying that followed! Or imagine even the practice calls — wouldn't they have had them, much as we moderns rehearse school fire drills? I think we can assume that the cliff people never suffered from boredom.

Or you may elect to go first to Casa Blanca in Arizona's renowned Canyon de Chelly, far into the Navaho Indian Reservation. It is even more spectacular, and harder to reach, with surrounding scenery that leaves you speechless. If you are doing the renowned Dam Detour across central Arizona, past Roosevelt and three other irrigation dams, you must surely stop at Tonto Cliff House, easier to reach than many. All told, our region of the cliff people has many hundreds of dwellings high up the sides of walls. Dozens have never been explored, and doubtless others haven't even been discovered. If you are a genuine explorer, you may hike or ride a horse back beyond the Four Peaks country or into any of several other mountain ranges and find a cliff palace which you may name for yourself.

Adele and I, on our honeymoon, had two months to go where we pleased. We chose the wilderness. One day we were caught in a rain and ducked into a cave. Next moment we discovered it was no cave at all, but one of those niches, not very high this time but holding remains of an ancient home, even to undamaged pieces of pottery and human bones. Go ahead, honeymoon at phony Las Vegas or some other garish "resort" where all you can do is spend money and pretend you are having a good time; Adele and I still think our Cliff Hotel is better, for somehow we established rapport with the ancients, we were one with God and Nature and Time.

As in the desert valley dwellings such as Casa Grande, the archaeologists have found many important things in the cliff homes — pots, implements, corncobs, weapons, woven fabrics, even dried foods. If you find such things you are honor bound to turn them in to some nearby museum, for they have no intrinsic value, they are not worthy as "souvenirs."

The cliff people themselves went to their homes as you must go, hand over hand, toes in little cracks. And they, mind you, carried babies on their backs, or pots of water and bags of grain. In the beginning they carried heavy rocks and mud for building. They walked to the forest, sometimes fifty miles distant, and brought back logs for *vigas* (VEE-gahs) or ceiling beams; it is partly through tree-ring studies (invented and developed at the University of Arizona) of these logs that our scientists have been able to date the dwellings. But exactly how they lifted such heavy objects to their castles fringed with sky, we can hardly imagine. There were never any formal stairways or steps. They may have used ladders, though in many instances there are now no landings suitable for ladders to rest on. They may have used hand-woven ropes to help pull their materials up, or to swing them down from the tops of cliffs. Remember, these ancients had almost no metals, and no wheels. For their day-by-day routine, going down to work their fields and back, going for water, bringing food and firewood, we must envision them shinnying torturously up and down the rock walls, dwarfed by the size of their cliffs and mountains into antlike size. Modern Navaho Indians still use the old toe holds to climb canyon walls in Canyon de Chelly.

Douglas Fairbanks, once a famous motion picture star given to acrobatics, climbed dramatically down from the top of a high cliff on a rope, swung vigorously, and landed in a dwelling that could not be reached from below. Erosion over the centuries had worn all the ancient toe holds away. Fairbank's idea, prompted no doubt by his press agent, was to be the "first white man" ever to visit this dwelling. It was a good idea as Hollywood ideas go, except for one thing: Fairbanks and his press agent found several cattle brands from nearby ranches burned on logs up there! Cowboys had long before swung down that same way, and left their usual signatures.

White people occasionally manage to get themselves killed trying to climb into cliff dwellings. So if you try, equip yourself with ropes, spikes, food, water, good shoes and clothing, first aid equipment, and good nerves. Don't try it alone, lest some explorer years hence be misled, on finding *your* dessicated form.

76

# VIII.  THE RED MEN

Actually it was a few short months ago that Adele and I sat in a Navaho Indian hogan in northern Arizona and enjoyed a meal of mutton, squaw bread, and coffee. Six members of that redskin family watched us, bug-eyed; except for the father, none of them had ever seen a white person before.

Arizona is still just that "wild." On the great wind-swept, snow-chilled mesas of northeastern Arizona, it had always been virtually impossible to make a living. So back yonder in the nineteenth century Uncle Sam herded all the 8,000 members of the Navaho tribe up there and in effect locked them in, fondly expecting, and hoping, they'd soon all die; the only good Indian was a dead Indian. But the nomadic Navahos, being stalwart men, adapted themselves to this impossible environment.

Thus by 1967 they numbered 100,000, had achieved a new dignity and respect, and were nowhere near starving. Many of them still live in mud-topped hogan homes of logs exactly as their great-grandparents lived, but the older ones are anxious for their children to receive a good education under modern white standards.

We can admire the Navahos, just as we can admire their neighbors the Hopis, and indeed all the other red tribesmen. Arizona is fortunate in having so many Indians in their native haunts, costumes and attitudes, and *you* are fortunate to be able to visit them. I hope you do visit them, to learn what manner of man faced extinction by the "superior" whites, yet survived, and grew.

## 1. Greatest of Them All

So, then, poor Lo the red man wasn't nearly so "poor" in spirit as many of us palefaces have envisioned him. For further proof, let us now go to that most warlike tribe of all, the Apaches, and discover the foremost Indian who ever lived. You think instantly of the murderous Geronimo? Of Cochise? Neither of those! This great one was a gentle person, shy and kind, and his astounding career is virtually unknown to most Americans. It was he who first pointed the red people toward white civilization; today they are profiting immeasurably by the work he did.

When President Theodore Roosevelt in 1906 asked him to head the U. S. Bureau of Indian Affairs, the Apache's name was Dr. Carlos Montezuma. But at his birth in the mountain wilderness of Arizona Territory he was called Wassaja (wah-SAH-yah). At age six, in the year 1871, he was tapped by fate.

In October of that year a band of Pima Indians, long victims of the predatory Apaches, found an Apache village unguarded. So just before dawn a hundred Pimas carrying pots of live coals and twists of dry grass swept out of darkness and set fire to the dozens of Apache wickiups. In a moment the whole village was aflame. Men, women, and children darted out of their homes screaming in panic. *Thwup!* The deadly arrow, no noisier than a rattler's strike, caught almost every fleeing Apache.

But the lad Wassaja ran naked across the flats there — until a Pima warrior on a horse gleefully reined up, grabbed him by the hair and lifted the boy up before him. It was the first horse the boy had ever seen, and he thought the warrior a part of the animal itself. He

78

expected to be eaten alive by the centaur, and so in sheer terror lapsed into unconsciousness. When he regained his senses he was a captive in the Pima's hands.

For weeks the victorious Pimas enjoyed torturing the Apache lad, but when that palled his captor took him into the white village of Florence and offered him for sale. A kindly bachelor saw him, an itinerant photographer named Carlos Gentilé. He opened his purse, took out thirty silver dollars — every cent he owned — and dropped them one by one into the scowling Pima's hands. The Pima demanded more, demanded horses. But he got none, and the sun was dropping low, so he rode haughtily away with his coins.

Carlos Gentilé took the still terrified red-brown boy to his church. There the minister said to the white man, "Your name is Carlos. And Montezuma is a famous name in the Southwest. Let us call him Carlos Montezuma." So christened, the Apache boy started life in the strange world of the white man.

It was stranger than our minds can envision. The hats, the beards, the clothing, the wagons, animals, harness, rifles, pistols, all were marvels beyond belief. The "tiny people" living on photographer Gentilé's wall would not speak, but only stare at him. The other Apache boy, singularly like himself, who lived in a funny window on the wall, would move and smile and grimace but never talk. The whites who crowded around tried to feed the captive everything imaginable — and all forgot to offer him water until he almost died of thirst. When he was bathed publicly at the town pump he thought that he would emerge as white as his owner, then cried when he did not. Finally, when the rough palefaces persistently teased and ridiculed the boy, gentle Mr. Gentilé put his "son" into his photo wagon and started on a long trek to the east. Though they faced grave and certain dangers they traveled alone, and went unharmed.

As they rode, the foster father taught. He was a cultured man, and infinitely kind. The lad learned new words, new wonders. The rhythm of the mules' hoofs became a beat for improvised music, far different from the chants of the wild Apaches. Reading and writing and, yes, arithmetic, were started, marvels all. God was created, though this took some doing.

When they eventually reached the end of the railroad at Trinidad, Colorado, the little Carlos saw his first iron horse. He was prepared for it, though he assumed it got its power from burning horses alive. Its fire-belching, screaming, ding-donging spectacle was truly a boy's delight. He in turn completely captivated the conductor, the other passengers, every person he met. Probably because of his ebullient health and Mr. Gentilé's intensive training, the lad already showed rare personality charm.

This grew right with him when they reached the Atlantic coast. There the two wagoned from New York to Florida and back across the inland regions, pausing to take photographs whenever they could. It was a wonderful gypsy life of loving and learning and growing up. Mr. Gentilé, richly educated, was a good tutor; but when they eventually reached Chicago he boarded the boy with a Baptist minister named Steadman in Urbana, to attend formal school. We do not know why loyalties were shifted from Catholic to Protestant, we know only that young Carlos became a staunch Baptist.

The Steadman family found bronzed young Montezuma a charmer. He was, flatly, the handsomest boy in town — a quick shy smile, a soft voice, inherent courtesy, with no hint of the "savage" left in him. Moreover, he was fascinated by the way paleface books captured not just words and pictures but whole wonderful ideas. He stepped out as leader of his class in school. If he had any problems as an adolescent there is no record of them. He moved from grade school marble champ — playing for keeps until Mr. Steadman intervened — to baseball expert in high school.

Late in this period, however, his benefactor left the boy's life as strangely as he had entered it. With no hint of anything but love between them, they simply lost contact. Gentilé had opened shop at 3907 Cottage Grove Avenue, Chicago — "Boulevarde Studio . . . Large Photographs By A Patented Process A Specialty . . . Horses and Carriages Photographed." He collected a valuable set of photos, including fine ones — which we still have — of himself and his purchased "son." He prospered; he joined the exclusive Chicago Press Club and for years his portrait hung on the wall there, tribute to his high reputation. Then in 1893 Carlos Gentilé died and was buried in the Mount Hope Cemetery.

Under Pastor Steadman's guidance and with help from the Urbana Y.M.C.A., the erstwhile savage lad entered a university. He was graduated as Bachelor of Science, *cum laude,* in 1884, just thirteen years after he had seen his first white man!

Meanwhile he was a good athlete, he taught Sunday School, sang in the choir and glee club, made speeches. He never courted girls, though they courted him. He worked in a drugstore owned by C. Pruyne Stringfield and there got a "taste" for medicine. But, more important, he had already acquired a crusader's zeal; as a college grad he felt it his life duty to help the red people who were his kinsmen.

"The Indian is spiritually and intellectually enslaved," the young man orated powerfully. "I am living proof that any red man can rise above his heritage. We must give my people a chance!" By "we" he meant the whites; he considered himself white now, though he also remained loyal to the reds.

He decided that the best way to help the Indians was to become a doctor, and with Mr. Stringfield's help went through medical school. On the day he won his M.D. the U. S. Government offered him a job as Indian agency doctor in North Dakota. Soon he was moved to Nevada. And at every step, now, indeed almost hourly each day, he was an aggressive champion of what he termed the Indians' cause.

"The policy of the government," said he, in public meetings, "is to insure jobs for the whites who work for the Indian Bureau. Any benefits to the red men are purely incidental. The red folk are no better off than they were fifty years ago!"

He was right, and coming from so picturesque a personage it made good newspaper copy. Editorials commented favorably, and soon he was much in demand for public speaking. Inevitably he became a thorn in the governmental flesh, and was hated by the white Indian Bureau personnel.

The Bureau countered by transferring him to the then American Siberia — an isolated post in Washington State, at Colville. His assigned work, as before, was simply that of agency physician, and a lesser man would have served out his time there, with a measure of security. Carlos Montezuma observed his red patients' ignorance and squalor, and he couldn't keep quiet.

"The Indian Bureau," cried he in one biting outburst, "consists of some seven thousand men and women, generally incompetent and broken down white derelicts, all drawing fine salaries from the hard-working taxpayers. The immediate executive authority for the Indian office is generally some party lame duck or political grafter called the Commissioner of Indian Affairs."

As he sounded off with increasing vigor he became intolerable as an employee of the very Bureau that he criticized. He was quietly "allowed to resign."

This created no stir, because he was already pointing toward a private practice. Now he set up office in Chicago, teaming at first with the distinguished Dr. Fenton B. Turck, one of America's foremost stomach specialists. "Monte" Montezuma — a nickname he liked — was now thirty-one years of age, a strikingly handsome bachelor of large bulk and quietly impressive manner.

In five years more he was the darling of Chicago's society set, serving the wealthiest people, but doing a monumental charity practice as well. He became a Master Mason and Knight Templar, he sang in church, he presided at meetings. In astonishingly few years he was wealthy, so that he pitched into his crusade with increasing zeal.

"We must have a regular audit of the Indian Bureau books," he orated. "We must make public details of how money is spent, and misspent. Graft must be ended.

"The dole system must be ended, the Indian educated so that he can support himself. He must no longer be shamed, a beggar squatting beside a reservation wigwam."

82

As the century turned, another irrepressible personality had galloped onto the American scene. This was Teddy Roosevelt, an enthusiastic outdoorsman, conservationist, and friend of all oppressed groups. He knew the West, and he sensed in Carlos Montezuma a kindred spirit. In 1906 he called the man to Washington.

"You raise a big smoke," grinned the President, "but there's a good fire under it. I read your speeches, study your ideas. I think you are basically right. You are a man of courage, Montezuma. So I want you to come here and be Director of the United States Bureau of Indian Affairs."

This news would truly have shocked some of his former Bureau associates. And it was a flattering offer, but Montezuma feared it might unintentionally be a way of fencing him in.

"Thank you," he replied humbly, "but I must stay close to the problem, close to my people, not sit idly at a desk in Washington."

Perhaps he decided wrongly. There are those who say, now, that Montezuma's acceptance could have advanced the very reforms he advocated by at least thirty years.

In 1916 he started a monthly magazine called — in memory of his Apache name — *The Wassaja*. In it he editorialized as militantly as he spoke. He named names and gave facts. He made specific recommendations for "giving the red man a chance" at white civilization.

But while his crusade aroused much high-level interest, with the masses it did not jell. Public apathy was profound; we were too close to the days of frontier warfare when "the only good Indian was a dead one." He was, forsooth, more of a nuisance than a prophet. This reaction undoubtedly hurt him more than he ever let on. Indians are "stolid"? They can be as hypersensitive as any white man.

Finally, in desperation he decided to take his crusade to the red folk themselves. He would "bust matters wide open" by arousing the reservations. To that end he went back to Arizona — his first trip "home."

Out of sentiment he hired a guide to drive him to the site of the village massacre where the Pimas had captured him. He talked to old men who had survived that bloody holocaust. He read the marvelous prayer sticks of the Pimas, on which was carved an authentic record of his capture and sale as a little Apache boy. He learned that his two sisters had escaped the carnage, with his parents, but that his mother Thilgeya had tried to flee the reservation in search of her little Wassaja, and had been cruelly shot down. He sat on a rock on Iron Mountain and cried bitterly. With great passion he yearned anew to help his kind.

Yet when he appealed to "my own people" the Apaches, they too scorned him.

"You can do as I have done," cried he. "You can rise high in dignity, prosperity, and pride. So, arise! Demand your rights. By mass action we can end the prejudice. I will lead you. Come!"

He spoke with great feeling, that first evening in the Apache camp; reminded the squinting, squalid reds that they were virtual slaves, told them of the American ideal that guaranteed freedom and equality for all, spoke to them of God and Christ the Savior. He would personally lead them upward, showing every step.

At the end, they laughed at him. He stood there, stunned. Not for a long while did he realize that they had flatly rejected him.

"He is no longer Apache, he is white," their spokesman jeered. "He has everything — food each day, a house, clothes, horses. So why does he bother about us? He is a fool. He is a crazy tom-tom beating for nothing. A doctor, he says. Dr. Tom-Tom-Beating-the-Wind! A fool!"

It was like that everywhere he tried. The reds simply had no conception of the missionary instinct; no understanding or sympathy for any selfless attitude. The white agency workers ordered him away as if he were a common whiskey peddler. Then their red charges ridiculed him even more.

Heartbroken, he went back to Chicago and resumed hard work. Hope sprang again, and he made other trips; but with the same results. He wrote more articles, made more speeches, to no avail. Church leaders and others endorsed him, but lent him little active support.

On a third trip to his homeland he took, at his own expense, Dr. Charles B. Gibson, a distinguished chemist and physician; George H. Morgan, a university classmate of Carlos, now a successful Chicago lawyer; Mrs. M. H. Davis, a magazine writer. He hoped they might somehow substantiate his own frantic appeals, might impress the Apaches where he alone had failed. They were as ineffectual as he.

At this period, too, he had another attorney in his employ, J. W. Latimer, stationed in Washington as liaison man with Walter L. Fisher, Secretary of the Interior. He was missing no bets.

"You are working too hard, burning too many candles," friends pleaded. "You'll kill yourself."

They were prophetic. But, said he, "Bosh!"

The only crumb of happiness in this period of his life — he was forty-eight now — came when Miss Maria Keller, a Hungarian, entered his office as a patient one morning. In their mutual loneliness they fell in love, though she was but twenty-three. On September 19, 1913, they were married.

"He was the perfect lover," Maria told. "We had much happiness. But for such a short time!"

One day in 1922 he came home and told her that he was going back to Arizona. At the train he gave her a flower in farewell, though he said little. She felt that he acted strangely. He was no longer the vibrant, forceful, determined Dr. Carlos Montezuma; he was suddenly a stolid Indian. She could not understand; she assumed that he was simply intent on his crusade and wanted to try the reservation once more. But Monte himself knew differently. For he had been ill, and had accurately diagnosed his own symptoms without giving Maria a hint. She knew nothing of tuberculosis.

He might have been cured in any of several good rest homes in Phoenix, but off the train there he hired a hackman who drove him out thirty-odd miles to an Apache reservation in the wildest part of the desert. He had no suitcase, only a small box. He paid the man, and was left on the desert alone.

Next he hired an Apache girl to build him a wickiup — the dome-shaped hut of the Apaches, made of tree limbs, grass, rags, whatever is available. He arranged for her to bring him food and water once a week.

Then this son of the Apaches, the young captive who had risen incredibly high in the white man's world, this champion of the mistreated Indians who had spurned him, stripped off his clothes, donned a G-string and lay down on the cold hard ground to die.

For weeks nobody but the Apache girl knew he was there. Then a Presbyterian medical missionary, Dr. C. H. Ellis, heard that "a strange old man" lay in a wickiup far from any human habitation. In Jesus's name he made a long trek to investigate. He was horrified at what he found. Here in a single blanket in a filthy, floorless hut lay a long stack of skin and bones, barely alive.

"Go away!" the bones croaked. "Go away now. I shall die here. Do not disturb me."

Dr. Ellis, compassionate, did not go away. He brought his canteen, and administered such aid as he could, having no idea whom he doctored. Then he saw a ring on the patient's finger. It held a gold and diamond Masonic emblem. Startled, he looked intently at the sick man's face, studied the shrunken features.

"My god!" exclaimed the missionary then. "You are Dr. Montezuma! What in the world are you doing here? I will get help at once."

He wired Maria and she rushed out. He contacted the Phoenix Masons and they went into action — or tried to. A government doctor was called in.

The sick man would accept no one, he rejected every effort to help him. Christmas turned, and he knew it not. He would no longer speak. He barely breathed. He would let no one touch him. A few older Apache men, learning about him, came around — and grinned. Dr. Tom-Tom-Beating-the-Wind was dying. He had had everything; he gave his life trying to help other people. He was a fool.

In a cold rainstorm that leaked through the poor thatch and onto the patient on January 31, 1923, just six days after wife Maria's arrival, Montezuma the mystic died.

The Masons from Chicago and Phoenix conducted his funeral, with a Baptist minister presiding. Thousands of persons — the reverent, the curious — came to the little chapel there at isolated Fort McDowell. Continuing rain cast an almost tangible gloom. And around the hills squatted some dozens of Apache Indians, looking on. These had jeered; these had rejected him when he had tried valiantly to help them, and when he pleaded for re-acceptance as one of their kind.

They could not know that he had laid a priceless groundwork for reform; that the changes he advocated for the benefit of the Indians were already quietly being started. As early as 1890 he was thundering, "All the Indians are *people!* They are citizens, they must be taught how to vote. They must have good schools, churches and homes, the same dignity that the whites enjoy. They must know our God. They must take their place as proud and patriotic Americans." By World War II most of those dreams had come true. By 1960 many latter-day champions, notably Senator Barry Goldwater, were echoing Dr. Montezuma's words.

About 1910 Dr. Tom-Tom was pounding for "Apache freedom." Said he, "Some tribesmen are farmers by nature, but others are not. My own people, the Apaches, should be taught ranching, not forced to grub in the soil or be given a handout. They are fine horsemen and could herd cattle with pride, for it is like riding to war."

He was scorned then. But in the 1930's his ideas took root, and in the 1960's the Apaches operate one of the greatest cattle ranching enterprises in America. They manage it themselves, teach their youth modern breeding methods, and have allied businesses for added income.

"There are vast ore deposits on the reservations," the crusading doctor insisted, "Coal and iron especially, and oil. These can be developed to bring the red people out of poverty."

It was so. By 1967 one tribe — which we whites had shoved onto an "impossible" desert reservation, hoping tacitly that their 8,000 members would quietly die — had 100,000 members in the richest tribe of all. Uranium alone made them rich, but there is oil, and other minerals. Moreover, they have caught the paleface ideal — when a white church sought to establish a mission hospital in isolated Monument Valley, the *Indians* gave $10,000 toward it! And through their tribal council these red folk, the Navahos, had set aside $25,000,000 as a rainy-day backlog — foresight no white government has shown!

Carlos Montezuma would have been delighted.

## 2. *Timeless Town*

But of course you cannot now visit Dr. Carlos Montezuma, indeed the feeling probably persists that all Indian life is a thing of the past. Actually, you can drive your luxury automobile right to the door of a hundred Navaho hogans or Apache wickiups this very day. Do come with me, here and now, in spirit, down a storied road both to yesteryear and tomorrow.

Specifically, let us turn north off Highway 66 and along a dirt road to the village of Ganado, through Keams Canyon, and finally to the most remarkable inhabited spot I know. Here are the Hopi Indian villages, literally cities in the clouds. Not "ruins," not vague mounds for the archaeologists' patient exploration, but sky towns with adults and children living the fullness of life as they have for untold centuries. Walpi, Polacca, Shungopovi, Oraibi, Hotevilla — their very names conjure up the mystery of the unknown. Here we can find the American Indian as he ever was.

It may be that you will approach from the west, via Flagstaff.

88

From there, drive due north on Highway 89 to a spot north of Cameron, and turn east again, to Tuba City, the government oasis at this side of the vast reservation area. Now you face the land of room enough, of crimson cliffs and purple canyons, a wild free world almost totally devoid of filling stations and cocktail bars. Here at Tuba, if possible, hire a Hopi or Navaho guide to go with you, perhaps a youth of high school age. It will be a treat to your party to have such a guest in your car, but don't make the mistake of being condescending. This guest, remember, was here before you were; you are on his own home grounds.

Oraibi offers no "Rooms To Let" (yet I have stayed there enjoyably in village homes). Into your car, therefore, put some blankets; this is the Painted Desert region, but not all deserts are warm, even in summer. A tent will be fashionable, but not essential. Food for four or five days is just routine caution. Leave rifle or pistol packed under the seat; Uncle Sam reserves hunting for the Indians. Pack in extra cans of water, gasoline, and oil.

They'll tell you when you get to Arizona that Old Oraibi was built in the time of Noah. And you will realize, after half an hour there, that it was surely ancient when Columbus sailed. The architectural motif was taken from the apparently boundless semi-desert all around. Thus the town is camouflaged, a part of the very landscape, until your car tops the hill and you suddenly exclaim, "Why those are not mere cliffs, they are buildings!" You will have climbed to a mesa, an astonishing sudden table-like upthrust of rock. Only a few acres in area, it will be hundreds of feet above the surrounding region, and you will immediately marvel at the choice of such a location. Your own reasoning will reply: these were, and still are, peace-loving folk who built here because it was the easiest way to defend themselves against predatory tribes. With no trees growing, they built of rocks that were at hand, and this has given permanence and beauty as well. Dwellings show erosion wrinkles in faded tones of gray, although a few now flaunt brightly painted doors and windows. There is no town clock, no whistle or bell to sound the hour, no constant pressure to hurry, hurry; no laborious intent on efficiency. There is not even rhyme or reason to the placing of houses, no thought of formal streets, for at Oraibi a man builds wherever he can find the spot for it, and if his dwelling is catty-cornered, who minds?

Sudden eyes will peer at you from around corners. A black head will rise behind a parapet three stories up — and duck back as quickly if you are caught looking. Walk, if you will, toward that mother and her brood, down the rocky path; the young will scurry up ladders and disappear like fledgling quail, and the woman will enter a door, look back through a crack and say in English, "No speak English."

This does not mean that you will be unwelcome in Oraibi. It means merely that you are not one of the Peaceful Ones, or Hopis, hence that it will take them time to size you up. If you are wise, you will use your wait to advantage. You will remember that this is a timeless town, and you too will do some preliminary sizing, noting that here are no chamber of commerce committees, no real estate salesmen, indeed no cafe, grocery, soda fountain, cocktail lounge, or jail. You will gradually see that these dwellings are jammed close in Manhattan manner, up on a sky island commanding a vast red plain. Not for half an hour, maybe, will even a dog venture out to give you a tentative sniff. Hold your peace, for events are forming. If you are the hurry-up kind of Yankee, you should not have come to Old Oraibi at all.

On my first visit I went boldly to a door and knocked. Nothing happened; nothing! I tried other doors and was similarly rebuffed. I walked the streets; the town was deserted. In exasperation I sat on a rock to think, for I was hungry and tired, and thirsty. After exactly thirty-one minutes a beardless and nearly naked ancient Father Time materialized from somewhere, came close to me, grunted, and sat down. By this time I was determined to outwait him, and in that village it wasn't easy. At 3:00 P.M. a sunny silence seemed to have stupified both of us. But at about 3:30 he held out a ripe peach.

Heaven may have some more delicious nectar, but I do not expect to encounter anything better on earth. The peach was both water and food, plus hospitality. The old Hopi nodded, understanding. He lifted his hand, waved it once slowly around. I think he meant the equal of our ranch folk's gesture when they say, "Welcome; what's ourn's yourn."

Next thing I knew, a lovely creature was coming down the little street. She probably was sixteen. She wore a sort of all-white costume, embroidered, with bleached buckskin leggings that made her moccasins look incredibly small. Her hair was hand-carved ebony, and a bracelet of silver and turquoise adorned her wrist. She carried a wicker basket filled with red pepper pods; her poise was magnificent. When she came alongside us, she turned and smiled. I arose and said: "I — I beg your pardon."

"You come to see Oraibi?" she asked. "It is all right. You will find it a very strange city. And the old one who brought you the peach is waiting for you to give him a coin."

"Oh!" Then I went on, foolishly, "You — do you speak English? May I —"

She laughed, not unkindly. Then we laughed together. She provided some conventional courtesies about the weather and traveling. Before I realized it, not two but at least ten Hopis had gathered. They appeared, I swear it, out of the rocks and walls. Some were children, broad-faced, slant-eyed little charmers, of apparent Asiatic heritage. One was a boy of about fifteen, one a woman of perhaps fifty, carrying a beautiful pottery bowl.

"I am named Mary Harper in English," the woman said. "I saw you come. We did not wish to intrude too quickly, but if you would like a drink of water — "

The bowl was in my hands, and I was drinking.

If you come without a guide, it is to be hoped that you encounter some Mary Harper when you arrive. How you do eventually "get in" with the Hopis is your adventure, and I can coach you only to use patience and common sense. Money is not the entering wedge, but here as everywhere it helps. The people are poor, by our standards; they are glad of a chance to show their town for pay, once their shyness is conquered and their dignity respected. You can even buy meals

91

in a home if you try tactfully. And if you like mutton! Lambs on the streets are as common as children and dogs; field glasses will reveal shepherds with flocks in the distant haze. You will surely be served mutton, stewed or roasted. A ewe slept in the room with us that night in Oraibi. "The smell of things here is not like the smell of things in white houses," Mary Harper said to me. She was a discerning woman, discerning both as to scents, and my discomfort.

You must remember in Hopiland that sewers and garbage disposals are comparatively new things. You must remember that, where water is cruelly insufficient, little will be available for frequent bathing, or washing down the streets.

"How is it," I asked an old Hopi wise man, "that you can throw your refuse out on the streets, where people live and children play? In cities, our children would soon be diseased."

He looked up worshipfully at the sun, lifting a hand as if in salute to that great god of the skyways.

"The heat, the sunbeams," he replied, "are sent to bless us. They kill that which would bring misery to our bodies." How right he was!

Try to beg, buy, or inveigle an invitation to live for twenty-four hours or longer in a typical Oraibian home. Luck with you, you can be there during a festival. By careful timing for August, you can be there in Hopiland for the renowned Snake Dance.

The Snake Dance is mentioned with bated breath, and it does truly live up to its reputation. For days a group of Hopi clansmen court divine favor by chanting and dancing with snakes — little brothers of the rain gods. The climax of their ceremony is incredible. In fantastic costumes, they grasp long live reptiles in their mouths and dance wildly. Most of the snakes are venomous rattlers.

"Don't they bite?" you ask, in awe.

Infrequently, but without a doubt, they do bite. And the dancers do not die or apparently suffer any ill effects. The snakes are not de-fanged or "milked" of their poison in advance, and what the Hopis do or take by way of immunizing against the poison is a tribal secret.

The Snake Dance is a religious ritual, as all Hopi ceremonials are. None of them is to be confused with our idea of dancing for pleasure, although a Hopi dancer has consummate grace and rhythm, plus inherent showmanship sufficient to keep him on a Broadway stage. The Kachina Dances, for example, are theatre de luxe on the village streets. In these the older clansmen appear masked and dressed like fierce Asiatic gods. Children are told that the Kachinas are the rain spirits here in person; when a child learns that they are really men of the village in costume, he is assumed to be mentally grown and is accepted in adult council. I watched the strange revelation evident in one small face as a father was identified.

"But they will bring rain anyway," this little boy assured me, a prying white. "The Kachinas always bring rain. They *are* the rain."

"Even though they are also men of the village?" I asked.

"Yes. Oh yes!"

"And even though you have attended white school, and know the white people's story of rainfall?"

"Yes. My father says it, and it is so."

Rain, you will learn, is all-important in this region. Water is a sacred gift, to be cherished. Comparatively little of it falls from the skies, but at the foot of the mesas are a number of ancient springs. Pedro de Tovar, sent out exploring by Coronado the *conquistador,* came to Oraibi in 1540 and discovered water issuing there. He also — wonder of wonders — found the Hopis burning black rocks; very few peoples ever of themselves discovered the usage of coal. Great deposits enrich the region from Tuba City to Gallup.

Water from the springs is carried up the long hills to the dwellings. Some of the overflow onto the plain is used to irrigate little gardens, and the fresh peaches you can expect in season perhaps will have been watered there. However, the Hopis are the best dry-land farmers in the world, too. In a climate that would convert other farms into dust bowls, these citizens manage to grow corn that is delicious, and beautiful to see. It is not the conventional white ears of the Iowa cornfields, nor yet the roasting ears of garden use. It is a mixture of bright crimson, bright yellow, maroon, and blue. The colors are grown in separate rows. Planting and cultivation are done by hands using a strong stick. Fields lie two miles — or twenty — away from the mesa citadels. I know one Oraibi citizen who grows corn twenty-two miles from his front door, and with his sons and friends goes there each day to work. And how do these Hopi farmers travel? Few horses are used, for a horse is too great a luxury. Listen, and be appalled. The Hopi farmers simply *run!*

Corn, to the Hopis, is another gift from the gods. Even the planting stick is sacred, and is buried with the farmer at his death. Sacred meal is sprinkled on the snakes at dance time. It is used at weddings, christenings, funerals, almost all other important occasions. And it is baked into the most extraordinary bread found in this hemisphere — the beautiful blue, red, or yellow paper bread called *piki.*

*Piki* is made of colored corn, powdered and mixed into a simple batter.The mother or daughter will swipe an extremely thin layer of it onto a flat stone, then stand that beside an open fire for baking. It turns into a "paper" like that of a wasp's nest, but for serving is rolled into a scroll or something like a loose cigar. Eat it, by all means, with the mutton stew or whatever else may be offered you, but don't try to take *piki* home. It's too fragile.

Oraibi craftsmen do some fine weaving of blankets, but mostly this village is noted for beautiful wicker baskets, ornamented with designs of flowers, eagles' heads, and such. Pottery seen there will be from the neighboring First Mesa, but it is exquisite and repre-sentative of these Peaceful Ones, with designs dating back hundreds of years. Tewaquaptewa, a leader who might have been Methuselah himself, told me his town was created when the first men appeared on earth. Who are we not to believe him?

# IX. SOUVENIRS

The typical out-of-state family, visiting our Grand Canyon for the first time, will park up there beside a pinon tree, rush to the rim, exhale "OO-o-o-o-ooo!" in cathedral tones — then hasten directly to the nearby souvenir stand. First of all, the good folk demand *proof of presence;* so they buy and mail an average of almost ten beautiful picture postcards each. Then they simmer down and hunt for something to keep for themselves. They may end up with literally anything from a ten-cent ash tray to a ten-thousand-dollar locomotive.

You think I'm exaggerating? No such thing. I saw a New Yorker dismantle, and ship home, a railroad locomotive that had served along our border in Indian warfare time. I have been hunting with two men who make a good living doing nothing but help wealthy guests catch mountain lions, alive. Dozens of professionals catch and cage rattlesnakes, Gila Monsters, and assorted other denizens for excited tourists. Hundreds of live burros (donkeys) are shipped out of state. Many of the things people buy are hideous and worthless because we act on impulse, yet the urge to buy souvenirs is nothing to be ashamed of. It simply needs guidance. Only you can decide what you want to cart away, of course, but I have seen too many buyers regret their purchases, not to provide you with a few warnings.

95

*Don't* buy impulsively. Your mind was conditioned, before you left home, toward the "buying mood" (which fact translates into a billion-dollar souvenir industry). Recognizing that fact, you can curb yourself and, to some degree, your family. The tendency will be to buy whatever is first shoved under your nose at the train window or in the filling station. The souvenir so offered may be quality merchandise, but may not. Take time, therefore, to look around. The better shops may be miles from your hotel, motor court, railroad station, or airport.

*Don't* buy knick-knacks. There are thousands of them, little doo-dads, gimcracks, gadgets, whatsits, things that soon clutter up your purse, then your suitcases, your car, and eventually your home. After just one week you begin to wonder why you ever bought them. You realize, very quickly on your trip, that they offer little of the culture of the region you visited, that you cannot show them with any pride to your friends, that they bring back few really stimulating memories. In short, you gypped yourself, and you feel a little silly about it.

*Don't* come with your guard up, prepared to "haggle." Somebody decades ago spread the rumor that all souvenir merchants are squeeze artists who will ask you four times the price of an article, then laugh behind your back if you pay it. This can be very true in such foreign lands as Mexico and Italy, notably; there, haggling is expected, appreciated and enjoyed by both parties. Not so in America, where dignity is cherished and honesty the common rule. Remember this, however: the very nature of their business makes souvenir merchants charge high prices. Souvenirs are luxury items; the selling season usually is short; the styles change frequently and an old stock can go dead on the shelves.

If your funds are limited, ask the reputable merchant to whom you go for his suggestions. He will usually go out of his way to be helpful. He will go back into his storeroom, up to his private office, anywhere looking for something that a discriminating and appreciative customer can afford. He will discuss the merchandise with you, pointing to its good and bad qualities, giving you its history, explaining its place in the southwestern scheme of things. I have seen this done hundreds of times, and I have seen the merchant many a time deliberately reduce his own price on some item in order to help a likable customer buy it. Shopping for souvenirs in such manner can be highly pleasurable. It is the only way to "haggle" successfully at all.

Books are the Number One souvenirs in the lower-priced field. Publishers are strict, and the public is stricter; the bad guesses in souvenir books (this usually means books of fact, instead of fiction) quickly disappear off the shelves, removed by the retailers because they do not sell profitably. Again, be guided by your merchant-friend. You want a book on lost mines of the Southwest? This one is delightful, makes repeat sales to the same people. This one is secondary, seldom repeats. You want a book on regional wild life? This one is more readable, but this one is more comprehensive in coverage. A book on Indians? A book about this state you have come to, or this town? Here it is. Even if you are just passing through, here is something to read en route, something of permanent value, something to keep in your home forever as a reference and a memory, something satisfying all around. And inexpensive. On any trip through the Southwest you should go home with at least six books of regional lore.

Postcards, too, can be well worth the collecting, especially if you specialize. In Arizona, you or your children can collect groupings of cactus and cactus flowers, of national parks and monuments (of which this state has more than all the rest of the nation combined), of city halls, of churches and schools, of varied scenery, of noted show places and historical points. Beware, if you let the children do this collecting; they'll end up knowing much more about the Southwest than you do.

Books and postcards, then, and what else?

Original paintings if you are interested, by all means. In the spectacular effects created by the southwestern sun on southwestern landscapes and faces, artists have found an earthly paradise. We have colonies of them by the score. You will find painters long established, and painters still unsold. To my mind, one of the great personal discoveries is of that unknown artist who, you feel, has exactly caught the spirit of the southwestern expanse, and sun, and color.

I'd do you no service if I tried to list many items. Wading with you through the jillions of ash trays, cactus lamps, and printed pillow tops and salt shakers and cowboy bandanas would exhaust us both, with small result. Cold, calculating analysis of the field, over some decades, convinces me that we must look to the Indians for our best sunland souvenirs. After your first week of excited interest, you too can settle down and ask yourself, "Now just what does most represent the difference of this region?" And "What can I buy without undue expense?" Inevitably you'll get around to the Indians.

Basketry and pottery may come first to your attention. It is doubtful if any race of folk anywhere ever made prettier baskets with scantier materials than the southwestern Indians. Some of these baskets are rough yet beautiful, many are as minutely perfect as is Mexican silver filigree. In design and form, the "pots" are equally important. A simple olla (pronounced O-yah) of rust-red clay, fired but porous, in a web of leather thongs or of woven grasses, and hanging from the roof timbers of some borderland patio, is for me the most beautiful and altogether satisfying object of pure decoration in our hemisphere. It is spherical, with a large curved-back mouth to admit a gourd dipper, for these ollas out here hold drinking water and keep it cool by evaporation through the clay. Its rich red color against a tracery of green vines, its gentle swinging in the breeze, all add to the harmony of the atmosphere in our patios. And yet, one warning: baskets and pottery often look absurd in the East, especially in houses built around 1910. Make sure you know just where your olla will fit in, before you buy.

But ahead of all other "souvenirs," I would recommend to you the rugs woven by Navaho women, and the precious silverwork of

Navaho men. Both, in strength and subtlety somehow combined, bear evidence of the vitality and deep spiritual certainty of a people long abused. Both will provide you with honest workmanship, and no trace of disinterest, or hurry.

Of course there are examples of adaptation to non-Indian ideals. I remember one particular specimen owned by C. H. Weeks in Phoenix. Someone had written to a trader on the reservation asking that a rug of the weaver's own design be loomed for him and sent C. O. D. He had chanced to write on his Elks stationery, from Lodge 492 at Ouray, Colorado, and so his rug eventually came to him bearing the bold design:

## B P O E 492

Another Navaho woman watched white men shoot each other in a range war in 1863, then wove three rugs on which she copied their several cattle brands. Collectors will sell their souls to get one of these rugs today. But more likely, it is the Navaho designs you will want to see. Hunt out Yeibichai rugs, on which the weavers copy sacred sand paintings of the Navahos — but with some minor variation, indiscernible except to the most experienced eye.

Other types of rugs with special reputations have developed in various areas about the 16,000,000-acre Navaho reservation, notably the Two Gray Hills rugs. It has no metallic colors, but has an intricate sophisticated pattern and a quality of workmanship hard to equal. All over Navaho country the weavers continue to develop and refine their traditional designs and techniques.

In the weaving of rugs no important faking has been possible; machine-made rugs just don't look Navaho-made. The Navaho weaver rarely uses the same pattern twice, rarely even makes two rugs of identical size. But she weaves conscientiously, with high pride, and lifetime wear may be expected of any genuine Navaho you buy. At the Chicago World's Fair almost four million people walked on two Navaho rugs after first stepping in sand, a treatment which would have destroyed most factory rugs in a few weeks. Those two needed only to be cleaned. They are in use now at Gallup, New Mexico, in perfect condition. But if the white man couldn't fake the weaving, he could imitate and substitute; hence some traders have stocked factory-made "western" rugs with what could be mistaken for Indian symbols. Shoddy things at best, they can be foisted onto easterners who are motoring through and are delighted at the picturesque Navahos squatting outside the trading post. More recently they have been turning up in retail stores throughout the country as "Arizona Indian rugs."

Cost of the wonderful, genuine Navaho rugs of course is a factor for all of us — and well it should be, in wonderful, capitalistic America. True, there is an element of society which says: "If you must ask the price of the yacht, you can't afford it." This is sheer cultural snobbery, as well as nonsense; money is our medium of exchange, and using it as our measure of excellence and quality is a convenient and honorable custom. It is so on Wall Street; it is so at our Indian Trading Posts. So — ask the price of the rug that catches your eye. If it is beyond your means, tell the trader — or the squaw if you are dealing direct — that you have only x dollars to spend, and ask what you can get for that. You may be agreeably surprised, and fortunate.

Rarity is the big deciding factor, because in modern times the dedicated Navaho women can earn more at other pursuits than they can by sitting long weeks at their looms. Look back now to the dust jacket or frontispiece of this book — at the exquisite painting of Indian Still Life by Earl Hammock. The background there shows a rug owned by Mr. Hammock. It is about six feet square and cost him $1,000, because it is done in the exquisite "herringbone" weaving pattern. Today there are only eight squaws left who can do this work. Colors here are from natural vegetable dyes, made by the weaver herself.

In my home at Phoenix are forty-two Navaho rugs. The largest is 10 by 14 feet, and it cost $2,500, twenty-seven years ago; today it is appraised at $5,000. Largest Navaho rug ever made was ordered in 1932 by a famous Indian trader, Lorenzo Hubbell, Jr. He first constructed a house of rock 40 feet long and 30 feet wide and 10 feet high, to hold the loom, which he made of pipe. Then he turned the work over to a fine Navaho woman called Julia Joe. She and her daughters Lilly and Erma rounded up and sheared 78 head of sheep, 60 white and 18 black. They spent two years processing the wool sheared from those animals, dyeing, carding and spinning it. They used a whole case of soap to wash the fleeces, and 288 envelopes of black and cardinal dye.

Then, with a pattern *firmly fixed in her mind only* (no drawn pattern of any sort is ever used by any weaver among the Navahos) Julia set to work. On most days she stayed at her loom from dawn until midnight. Three years and three weeks after she sent the first spindle through, she ran a tiny thread out the border to the outer edge. This was important — that thread to the exterior, as in all good rugs, lets any evil spirits out (and who among us would want an evil spirit cooped up on our living room floor!) That signaled to everybody that her rug was finished.

It was, and is, and probably will forever be, the largest Navaho rug ever woven. It is verily a masterpiece of design and technique as well as of size. It measures 26 by 36 feet, is seamless and weighs 250 pounds. It is in delicate color and symmetrical design. It has since been exhibited throughout America, notably at the New York World's Fair.

At this writing, Julia Joe is aged ninety-one. She says that Lorenzo Hubbell gave her "a box full of money" for her work, and she was happy with that. At finishing time, the rug was priced at $20,000; today after inflation — had you heard of this phenomenon? — it probably is worth twice that. Buy it, if you can; by the year 2000 you may own a $100,000 rug.

White fashion designers have drawn on Navaho religious symbols in making costumes for women and girls. Sometimes the symbols are hand-painted on white cloth. For a more striking effect,

101

the symbols are beautifully sewn in the four main colors of the Navaho legend — blue, red, black, and white. Typically, symbols of the morning god, or Yei, enhance a simple off-white linen dress. The evening god, the rainbow god, and the lightning god also may be seen on clothing made by the palefaces. Older Navahos take a somewhat dim view of this appropriation of their symbols, suspecting the whites of at least a limited reverence and respect. But a younger "mod" generation that has had white schooling says "Why not? Copying our stuff is a compliment." Maybe they have a point.

A genuine Navaho bracelet may be made ninety miles from a town or railroad, its silver tediously, lovingly, melted and poured, hammered and annealed, formed, filed, stamped with hand-made dies, trimmed and polished to perfection. It will probably be heavy, and it will be unlike any other ever made. But in late years large concerns have mechanized production of a cheaper silverwork, in critical competition with this fine primitive art. Such mechanization is not necessarily dishonest, but the product is not Indian, or individual.

One promoter has developed a factory where fifty men are stamping designs and mounting stones on thin silver in assembly-line manner. Five thousand bracelets may come through in exactly the same pattern. The forms are made by a press or drophammer or by casting, which eliminates 90 per cent of the handwork while producing an inferior product. A good Navaho bracelet of heavy silver, with all the enduring quality and charm for which the hogan smiths are famous, may retail for $50; a flimsy machine-made copy of it can be profitable at $10. The average tourist, in first flush of admiration, is not aware of any difference. Some factories even label their output "GENUINE INDIAN design JEWELRY," three words in large type and one word very small. Indian hands probably never touched any item bearing such a legend.

The income to all the Navaho smiths from their jewelry in one recent year was about $70,000; but in one year an estimated $1,500,000 was paid for spurious Navaho jewelry in Hollywood and

Santa Barbara alone, with other outlets in proportion. New York City, two thousand miles from the reservation, paid an estimated million.

Even the turquoise jewel that looks so gorgeous is nowadays likely to be merely a piece of dyed sandstone. Recently a salesman in Phoenix was offering Indian stores large pieces of "turquoise" for fifty cents. It was beautiful stuff, but if you applied even a little heat it would ooze paraffin dye, and a fingernail would scratch it. Most dealers turned it down; nevertheless it appeared in jewelry in one retail market within thirty days. Your protection against such substitution is to make local inquiry for names of reputable merchants, who can guarantee genuine Indian manufacture.

Good turquoise is a hard stone showing "the blue of the sky and the green of the growing corn," with considerably more of the former. Once in a great while its beauty is enhanced by a natural tracery or "spider web"; little of this has been found in recent years, so if you own a piece wear it with special pride.

Both Navahos and whites buy more bracelets than all other jewelry pieces combined. The best are heavy, with little flexibility. Thousands of male westerners — who would disdain any hint of femininity in their apparel — wear Navaho silver and turquoise, often in matched sets. But I have one story, nevertheless, to tell concerning Arizona ignorance of this fine Arizona product.

Lieutenant Melvin D. Rogers came through the Navaho reservation to Tucson, Arizona, and went into a drugstore for ice cream. A girl soda jerker saw his hand, and her eyes went wide. She hastened back to the store manager — this being in war time.

"T-There's an escaped German prisoner at the counter!" she whispered excitedly. "He's in American army uniform, but he forgot to take off his swastika ring!"

"Take no chances," the manager ordered. "Stand back and let me handle it."

The lieutenant, an easterner, was duly "captured" — and the Arizonans are still embarrassed because they didn't know the Navaho swastika. This antedates Hitler by centuries, and is a common symbol on both rugs and jewelry. Hitler's swastika reversed the Navahos' as a mirror does.

Other standard patterns are raindrops, stars, crescents, crosses, arrows, sunbursts, whorls. For years all jewelry was relatively crude because the smiths had only coarse files. Today, a good smith will have twenty to fifty hand-made dies. He will apply his pattern in geometric precision, seldom with any measuring or spacing beyond that of his eye.

Navaho men, women, and children often wear small fortunes in their own tribal jewelry, whether at home or in town. This quantity display — perhaps a dozen bracelets, six rings, earbobs, a concha belt, two or three necklaces, studded bridle and saddle — is invariably in good taste. Many of the girls wear comparable quantities of silver. Navaho jewelry grows on you with its strange beauty; it can heighten the effect of almost any costume.

Navahos use their jewelry for buying goods, paying debts, and pawning. Rarely is a piece not redeemed, but if a white customer can buy any "old pawn" jewelry he has something of exceptional value. Those products of the hogan silversmiths, and those rugs woven by their squaws, have been referred to as America's only crown jewels. Certainly they have come from our own soil, and are the finest things I know now being produced by any of the aboriginal Americans. If such artistry comes to an end, we shall all be losers.

# X. OUR PIONEER PADRES

## 1. Tumacacori

Most of us Americans, especially those born east of Texas, were told that America was founded on the Atlantic seaboard.

"The Pilgrim Fathers who landed at Plymouth Rock were the first white people to establish a permanent colony in what is now the United States of America." This is an exact quotation from a school reader. It is downright inaccurate, even though it reflects a common belief.

Actually, America was pioneered not in the northeast but in the other geographic extreme, the southwest. Long before the Pilgrim Fathers sailed from England, generations of settlers from Spain had come into the sun country stretching from New Orleans to San Diego. Years before the good ship *Mayflower,* Europeans had created roads, ranches, towns, schools, even a newspaper, down here in the sun-bathed zone.

"But our Pilgrims came because of religion," one easterner told me. "Your Southwest was pioneered by conquerors out to find gold."

Wrong again. The Spaniards built a magnificent series of churches, for the Indians as well as for themselves, from that same

105

New Orleans to that same San Diego, and even on up the Pacific Coast another five hundred miles. True, our *conquistadores* came in search of treasure — but who rode literally at the head of each procession? Who guided Coronado, that greatest treasure hunter of all? A priest!

The gold hunters didn't find the legendary Seven Cities of Cibola which they sought, and didn't find much other treasure worth mentioning; so they went on back to Mexico City, to Madrid, and elsewhere. But the padres stayed; the pioneer padres, bald devout men in black robes, flaunting no blunderbuss or sword but holding high a cross, with it alone defying the murderous Apaches. More came, and more, and with them settlers for Christian communities.

These early Spaniards brought negligible tools and no materials for building, but they erected churches that have changed the course of empire. In this, our sun-baked rainless country, their massive and mud-built missions still stand, are still in use, hoary and hallowed by the centuries of grandeur. California's chain of missions is famous, as indeed is the Alamo, and that ancient church near El Paso in Juarez, those lovely churches of New Mexico, and at least two missions in Arizona.

You who are re-discovering the Southwest, or who perhaps are visiting here for the first time, must take time to visit at least one of those missions. Don't plan it as a momentary stop between 11 A.M. and lunch. Instead, try to give over one day, or several hours at least, to the seeking of a mood. Try to choose a day when there will be no crowds, when you can sit in the patio, in the sanctuary, in the cloister or yard, and relax. Try, above all, to project yourself back to those heroic times when the missions were new, and life held interests far different from ours.

To that end, I always like to visit ancient Tumacacori. It is located on a paved highway eighteen miles north of Nogales, Arizona-Sonora. It is a ruin, unused for many long decades. It is seldom overrun with tourists. The region around it is not populous, but is

106

still virtually as wild as when the first padres laid the first adobe bricks.

Most of the original structure remains, and just enough restoration has been done to show you the marvels of its architecture and decoration, and to suggest the routine of mission life. A new museum has been built nearby. Even if you are not especially religious you can respond to the place; for one thing it has an alluring lost-treasure legend. Tumacacori has an air about it, a feel of mystery. The winds of memory and the ghosts of yesteryear consort there hour by hour, and you can, if you wish, join in their strange fiestas. Tumacacori can well serve as representative of all the pioneer missions, if you have time to investigate but one.

In restoration, methods as nearly as possible like those of the original builders were used. Bricks were made on the grounds, and great logs brought from the nearby mountains and hewn by hand. Today the place looks alive from a distance, then gradually discloses its ruin as you approach. The front tower roof is missing, but the original facade of the nave is still impressive. Some walls are as much as nine feet thick. This was because Tumacacori served as both fortress and church. Many wooden beams are as good now as they were two hundred years ago.

White ranchers, in Civil War times, began stealing Tumacacori's adobe bricks, and some of the old timbers, for use in building their own homes. But local Mexicans and Indians still regarded the place as sacred. One slaying took place when a crass Yankee started to remove a beam that supported one of the tower bells. Indians had been awaiting him, it is told; they sprang out of the shadows, high in the tower, just as he began his thievery. When they killed him, they dropped his body through the bell archway down to the hard ground.

The adobe bricks were sun cured on the site. For centuries adobe has been the choice building material of the arid Southwest; my own Arizona home, erected by Indians, is of bricks exactly like those at Tumacacori. The technique of making these bricks was derived from North African Moorish influences, by way of those

107

first Spanish pioneers. Our Indians had used adobe clay for centuries, but had puddled it as thick mud and piled it up layer by layer. Spaniards taught them to mix straw with the mud, as a binder, then sun-bake it in convenient slabs or "bricks." In the 1540's, when the first padres came in and began their teachings, Indians mixed the straw in the mud by tramping it with their bare feet. Indians hired by my contractor mixed the mud and straw for my adobe house by tramping it with bare feet. They put the mixture in molds 4 by 12 by 18 inches and let it cook for three months in the summer sun; then the slabs were ready for laying into walls.

That name Tumacacori means "slanting rocks," from a nearby site where Nature has thrown earth's rocky strata at an angle. All about are rolling hills with valleys sloping down to the green-fringed river. But most growth here is cactus, chaparral and mesquite, the latter that hardy arid-land tree which furnishes pods of edible beans. Such growths nearly always indicate adobe soil. Adobe for my home was found by removing three feet of topsoil in the back yard, but topsoil in the Tumacacori area often is barely three inches.

Fine color tones were applied to the mission inside and out. On some walls were painted gorgeous roses. Everywhere the lines of the place show that the padres had an eye for beauty as well as strength, employing solid massive walls, domes, vaults and arcades, all built with only untrained Indians for help.

The new museum is so much in harmony with the old mission structure that in its patio you can readily project yourself into the past, if you have a knack for meditation. The museum is one of America's finest, arranged as all museums should be — not as a mere warehouse to store glass cases of exhibits, but a re-creation of the environment it preserves. There, in authentic mission architecture, is a fireplace which might be the very one at which Padre Kino warmed his hands. Floors, walls, ceilings, the very mood and atmosphere of the place, are Tumacacori as of yesteryear. This one building, in fact, is claimed to be the only authentic restoration of the architecture of the Spanish missions in our Southwest.

108

Many of the tools and utensils used by the missionaries are there for you to handle. Many fine art studies and photographs are on display. Around the walls of the main rooms are dioramas which bring the old life back in miniature. Stand before any of these for two minutes and you will have lost two centuries. Father Kino and his Indian guide are shown exploring the desert country, and the first few cattle which he brought to Tumacacori in 1697 are drinking from a water hole. The horses, men, cattle, cactus, water, the whole landscape, are perfect, as are the details in the next extraordinary diorama, which shows an Indian attack. In the siege a priest is shown trying to defend a home in 1751. Arrows are flying, destruction is shown. A man is sprawled, dying, and a woman kneels in prayer. Down to the tiniest detail even of facial expression and color, the figures are lifelike; it is hard to realize that they are but miniatures scarcely eight inches tall. These dioramas were made by a group of specialists in the National Park Service who have done similar work for other parks.

Foremost among the dioramas is that which shows you a later Tumacacori, as of perhaps 1700. I have stood before it half an hour, spellbound. You will see the interior of the place reproduced in miniature to exact three-dimensional scale, in precisely the detail and colors that were used in the actual building. The very candles, an inch tall, have flickering flames. Before you will be a large congregation of Indians and Mexicans kneeling at mass. Costumes, hair, hands, fingernails, facial features including lowered eyes, all details combine to perfect reality. Whatever your faith is, you will be awed; you will not want to speak, only to look and wonder. Then presently, when the room has become very quiet, from nowhere will come the incomparable notes of the Gregorian Chant. The Choir before you has begun singing! And you yourself have entered the scene, Liliputian, enthralled.

The music is striking evidence of the exactness and detail with which our National Monument men have sought to re-create the mission's heyday for us. No maker of phonograph records in America

109

had a recording of the Gregorian Chant exactly as it would have sounded a century or more ago, and no choir here was equipped to make such a recording. But through a firm in Paris, which has made a specialty of sacred and historic music, the precise intonations and shadings were recorded. Now when you stand a few moments before the diorama, long enough to project yourself into the scene, a museum guide touches a secret button and the Chant begins, at exactly the right volume. You do not see the mechanism, you only hear the glorious sound. I have never known better theater.

Through the museum side doors, go onto the porch made by colonnades, where walls are tinted sky blue and massive archways lead into the patio. Here you'll find the same shrubs and flowers that the padres knew. Here you can sit for hours and re-populate the place with fascinating folk of another day. You may, in your imagination, see the black-robed priests moving along the flagstones, the Indian workmen carrying huge beams for the mission roof, their children perhaps playing games with mesquite beans, even a lovely senorita watching her reflection in the patio pool. You will wonder why some Hollywood genius has not come to stage a screen classic built around the mission romance.

It is a well known "fact," for instance, that on yonder spot under that very same tree, in 1746, beautiful Dolores del Saenz listened to the courtship of a young English-colonial adventurer who rode through the Southwest, only to see him killed on the spot by a jealous Spaniard. The bloodstains of the handsome hero may be shown to you, on that rock where he fell with Dolores weeping over him.

When you lift your eyes to the majesty of Tumacacori today, a guide will tell you that the bell tower does not have the original two bells. Where are they? The bells have been added to the treasure legend. A stranger came unannounced out of Mexico a few years back and said, "I know where the sacred bells are buried, I can show you the place." Missing no bets, our government men went with this volunteer guide. They came back with two clappers, and later in the

110

same area found one bell shattered to pieces. Of the inscription originally on its rim, the words "Santa" and "Anno" were still legible. But where is the other of the two bells of Tumacacori?

"The sacred jewels were packed inside one tower bell and sealed there for burial when the Indian wars became unendurable," says the legend now. But — burial where?

When Spain withdrew financial support from the New World missions, Tumacacori along with many other churches had to be abandoned. Some gesture at using the place was made as late as 1830, but travelers in the gold rush of 1849 often camped there and reported it already in ruins. Others passing by, Mexican soldiers, Pancho Villa the great *insurrecto,* and Pershing who pursued him, all camped there, but Tumacacori's quiet survived them.

Today you can still see evidence of the treasure seekers. They carved names and dates on the walls; the urge to do this apparently is as old as Man himself. Tom Bourgeois, a French prospector, in 1900 built a house out of the old dormitory walls adjoining the main mission, and set himself up as fierce guard over the place. When the government took over the mission Tom grew morose and moved up into the Santa Rita hills. Humble natives say that Tom was decapitated by Indians, and that "On a moonlit night, *señor,* you can see a headless man riding a horse and carrying away the padres' treasure in a bag."

Of course I had to lie in wait for that headless one, and sure enough in the mystic moonglow one evening there he came! The night was chilly, so he had a shawl wrapped around his neck, and since he wore no hat his silhouette did indeed look headless. But the bag of treasure was a short shovel in a piece of canvas, for this was — ah me — a prosaic water tender working the night shift on irrigation canals.

Bats adorn the inner walls and ceilings of the mission. Doubtless they are the ghosts of which local superstition tells, creatures that add an eerie life to the old monument, otherwise so silent. It is a good idea to sit nearby, alone, when they come streaming out at sundown.

111

Wait, if you will, for the first stars through the archways; conjure back those who came here centuries ago to work and fight and love and dream, then harken as the wind whispers over their nearby graves.

Thus surely you will find, not gold, but the higher treasure that is the spell of ancient Tumacacori.

## 2. In Old Tucson

We cannot dismiss the pioneer padres, the Spanish or Mexican stalwarts who opened our state, without reminding you that they also developed what to my thinking is the most romantic city in this nation; not the biggest or the best and surely not the prettiest, but the one with the most intriguing legend. In recent years a new generation of moderns has foolishly tried to forget the past and make this city a competitor for ultra-sophisticated Phoenix, and that is cause for sorrow, because theirs had so *much* of true glamor to build on. The padres started it, and the languor-loving Latins set the pattern for a happy life. They built a wall all around it to keep predatory savages out, then set up a life for living and loving and letting the rest of the world go by. You can see an authentic replica of that walled town a few miles out from the modern city, and do go there by all means, to dream again, to see what we Arizonans had, and lost.

It is not within the scope of this book to profile the modern city for you, but truly you are encouraged to go there and seek out those who love it for what it was. Talk with them over patio tea, under the mesquite shade. You will sense the pervading feel of culture, which not even the moderns could kill; the appreciation for art and music and drama and literature, all the sweeter nuances of human existence. Try to find a few dark-skinned citizens and encourage them to talk; you'll catch a glimpse of romance again, genuine romance.

112

In our state's history one woman sensed that romance best of all, and was able to give it some sort of permanence. She was that same Sharlot Hall, whose poetry is quoted earlier in this volume, the little girl horse wrangler who grew up in this state — territory then — and was responsive to all its offerings of beauty. *She* saw the old city, *she* learned of its background, and left us this memory:

In old Tucson, in old Tucson
How swift the happy days ran on!
How warm the yellow sunshine beat
Along the white *caliche* street!
The flat roofs caught a brighter sheen
From fringing house leeks thick and green,
And chilis drying in the sun;
Splashes of crimson 'gainst the dun
Of clay-spread roof and earthen floor;
The squash vine climbing past the door
Held in its yellow blossom deep
The drowsy desert bees asleep.

By one low wall, at one shut gate,
The dusty roadway turned to wait;
The pack mules loitered, passing where
The muleteers had sudden care
Of cinch and pack and harness bell.
The oleander blossoms fell,
Wind-drifted flecks of flame and snow;
The fruited pomegranate swung low,
And in the patio dim and cool
The gray doves flitted round the pool
That caught her image lightly as
The face that fades across a glass.

In old Tucson, in old Tucson,
The pool is dry, the face is gone.
No dark eyes through the lattice shine,
No slim brown hand steals through to mine;
There where her oleander stood
The twilight shadows bend and brood,

113

And through the glossed pomegranate leaves
The wind remembering waits and grieves;
Waits with me, knowing as I know,
She may not choose as come or go —
She who with life no more has part
Save in the dim pool of my heart.

And yet I wait — and yet I see
The dream that was come back to me;
The green leek springs above the roof,
The dove that mourned alone, aloof,
Flutes softly to her mate among
The fig leaves where the fruit has hung
Slow-purpling through the sunny days;
And down the golden desert haze
The mule bells tinkle faint and far;
But where her candle shone, a star;
And where I watched her shadow fall —
The gray street and a crumbling wall.

## 3. Modern Missions

You must not leave this chapter with the feeling that everything concerning Arizona's missions is old, outdated, in ruins. We see the fascinating physical remains of the buildings erected by our pioneers, and tend to think they belong to a forgotten era. Actually, the men and women who served there set the pattern for decency and culture which still holds. Moreover, the pioneer missionaries were by no means all Catholic. Many Protestant denominations had their representatives in here, right with the immigrants from the east. Their tracks are still deep, and clean. The Methodists, the Baptists, the Christian Reformed, and surely the Presbyterians, are especially to be praised for their valiant work among early-day Indians and whites alike.

The Presbyterian mission at Ganado — away up northeast in the Navaho country — became world renowned. For a long time it was the only spot that offered a doctor or a hospital bed within many miles. It was small and ill equipped when a medical missionary named Clarence Salsbury was sent there to fill in a vacancy "for a few months." He stayed more than twenty years, built a big new hospital, established a school for training Indian and other nurses, built a high school, generally upgraded the whole life and outlook of the "savages" around him.

Such institutions, Protestant and Catholic alike, were not mere "sin killer" oases in the wilderness. They set high standards of education, too; standards also of community service; standards of selflessness, which is the Christian ideal. Culture was introduced along with the seeds of Christianity, and both flourished, particularly in the Navaho children in the boarding schools. The fruits of these efforts are seen today in the fact that by far the largest percentage of the dynamic leadership in the rapidly progressing tribes are the products of our mission schools.

The work of the pioneer padres and preachers was never easy. Often it was frustrating, discouraging; and often still is. But results show, sometimes when least expected. An incident in the life of Dr. and Mrs. Salsbury is significant, and typical.

They had been at Ganado for more than a year, doctoring and preaching and teaching and working hard. One day they were crossing the wild reservation in an old car in a rain, when they came to a swollen stream. Dr. Salsbury felt low in spirits.

"We seem to be wasting our time in this job," said he, to his wife. "I have preached and pleaded here for a year, and I can't think of one single soul I have brought to Christ. The Indians just listen, and say nothing."

He got out of his car morosely, to stare at the water in the stream. He decided it was safe to cross. Over yonder on the other side, he noted, was a Navaho man on a horse, apparently waiting to cross in the opposite direction. They waved to each other through the rain, then Doc got in his car and chugged into the water.

It was deeper than he had thought. Suddenly, grave danger

115

faced him and Mrs. Salsbury; the car was being pushed sideways downstream, was about to be turned over. Several yards separated them now from either bank. They were trapped in midstream, with water at the speed of rapids. Terror assailed them.

In the storied nick of time, that Indian untied his lariat rope, built a loop and tossed it. He caught the radiator ornament on the old car. With the other end of his rope snubbed around a big rock near him, the Indian held the car fast in the stream while Dr. and Mrs. Salsbury followed the rope across to safety, soaked but grateful. The Indian had plunged in to help them, risking his own life.

When the thanks were all said and the danger was over, Dr. Salsbury turned to his Navaho friend and spoke frankly. "Why did you bother to help us? We are palefaces, traditional enemies of the redskins. Yet you risked your life to save ours. What made you do that?"

The red man looked at the white missionary and explained — "You make good talk about Jesus. Me believe."

116

# XI. RED HOT

IRONS

The five most picturesque actors ever to perform on the American stage are — in the order of their appearance — the Indian, the trapper, the prospector, the Mexican, and the cowboy. Happily, *all* of them have performed with distinction in Arizona and *all of them are still here,* still going through their paces, still speaking their lines. Any day you may shake hands with them in a friendly visit.

But of the five, one of course is an all-time standout, a Hero among heroes. Through a century of fiction, motion pictures, radio and television he has galloped grandly across our consciousness, adventuring under the southwestern sun. But deeper than that, he also has functioned magnificently in the harder world of fact. He is not a figment of fancy, he is real! Americans consume millions of tons of red meat every year; steaks and roasts hacked off the carcasses of cows. Just who do you think manufactures that meat? It may reach your hands in the local deluxe supermarket, but it was originated by an old whanghide laborer out on the open range. And if you are wise at all in Arizona, you'll make the opportunity to go out there and talk with him. The cowboy probably is the smartest all-around business man we have, when you consider such priceless intangibles as personal freedom, friendliness, and philosophy of life.

If you show even average friendliness in turn, you'll get into a talk-swap that's immensely rewarding. And if you want unforgettable history, steer the cowboys into stories of cattle brands. Let's sample one such Arizona drama right here:

There was a standing reward of $500 for anybody who caught a cattle rustler, but Tom Reid, age twenty-two, had given it no thought. His chin dropped when he rode unexpectedly onto two men stealing his dad's steers. As usual in modern rustling, they were driving the fat animals into a big motor truck. One man saw Tom and ran toward a rifle leaning against one of the truck's wheels.

"You better leave that gun right there!" young Tom warned, and though he looked boyish, his voice didn't sound so. Moreover, from his saddle pocket he had produced a .45 pistol, the same old heavy hogleg his dad had given him, secondhand, to shoot at coyotes.

One rustler was standing still, but the other was inching toward the rifle.

BANG!

The rustler's gun fell flat on the ground.

"I aimed at a rifle and hit it," Tom said. "I could just as soon aim at your belly. I ain't jokin'."

That occurred on Tuesday. On Saturday I dropped in at the Reid ranch house for late supper. And for telling me about Tom, Mrs. Reid could hardly set out the victuals.

"Tom's right proud," said Mrs. Reid, who was right proud herself. "He's already got the reward money, and his pa deeded him 500 acres to start out on his own. Pa's so happy — law me! Tom's already got his own brandin' iron made. Show what it burns, Son."

118

Tom's father held a piece of calf hide on the hearth while Tom heated the iron red hot in the fireplace. In a moment he slapped it on. There was a sizzling sound and the acrid smell of scorching hair. When Tom removed the iron, the hide showed this brown-black symbol:

## 4 5

"You see," Mrs. Reid explained, "Tuesday — the day Tom caught up with the rustlers — was his pa's forty-fifth birthday. And since he used the .45 pistol his pa gave him and all, Tom figured a '45' brand would be right appropriate. Now, I say a brand had ought to . . ."

And so until late in the evening we sat there and discussed cattle brands. Here, right under my nose, was a brand and a new ranch being created by a young American whose heart held both courage and kindness. And here, from the minds of the elder Reids, whose roots are deep in the western range-land, came a treasure of branding legend and lore.

They will tell you anywhere in Arizona that a branding iron is forged not of metal but of sentiment. I have had occasion to investigate that premise, and I found that it is definitely true. The incident at the Reid ranch is not the most sensational on record, but it is typical. Two thieves, a gun, and a father's birthday; adventure, danger, family love. Mix these together, and from the resultant emotions' influence on the imagination comes a new design in iron to be recorded indelibly on steers' hides.

Since about 2000 B.C. (the earliest known era of fire branding) literally millions of brands have been designed. Most of it has been done in America, for here cattle raising became more than a secondary pastoral industry. With the opening of the West, the vast plains and mountain areas, from the Mississippi to the Pacific, were suited best to the raising of beef, and still are. Nowhere else has stock raising ever reached such epic proportions. Nor is it a fading glory, as we often hear; more people like more beef today than ever before, and the trend is likely to continue.

In practical use, to be sure, a brand is merely an identification mark such as you would ink on your laundry. Many ranchers have seen it only as that, holding in their souls no precious spark of imagery or beauty. Many more, though, have held that spark, notably in Arizona.

Consider the young Tormeys. They came West as bride and groom. They had worldly effects — wagons, horses, tools, guns, money — but most of all they had love. This love, they had pledged, should endure. It was the dominant thing in their eager young lives. So it was only natural that young John Tormey designed, registered, and for five decades used this brand:

And do you think Nancy Tormey cherished it? She shot the Apache Indian who, a split second later, would have crashed his tomahawk into her husband's scalp. She bore six sons and four daughters. She outlived John four years, and one of her last acts, as an enfeebled but proud great-grandmother, was to sew the beloved Two Hearts brand on a beautiful new bed quilt.

Before campfires or fireplace coals, far from cities and paved highways, I have heard of many sentimental brands. One of these was another heart brand — this time a single heart divided irregularly across its middle. It belonged to the Lennox ranch. It, too, had its source in a love story, but one with an ending that differs from the Tormeys'. When still a bridegroom, young Mr. Lennox succumbed to some inner weakness and he deserted his wife and fled with a Mexican girl. Mrs. Lennox did not pine or perish, for hers was an era and an environment in which women had to be strong. She herself went on with their original plans. She slaved and fought and suffered and triumphed, building, from almost nothing, a ranch of 40,000 cattle, each one bearing in its time the Broken Heart brand.

In lighter vein is the equally true story of the charming Lillybelle Plunkett. I say "charming" because she must have been. When she came West with her father to set up a ranch, cowboys in that country began courting at once. Their way of paying tribute was to rope any maverick (an unbranded calf or cow), topple it beside a fire, and with running iron brand a huge LIL on its side. Then they would take it to the young lady as a gift. Rivalry in this practice soon became intense.

Miss Lillybelle accepted the gifts and smiled at the givers — spiritual manna, indeed, for cowboys in a nearly womanless region. In a short time her LIL herd had grown to valuable proportions. But did she then select one of the romantic cowboys? Not Lil! She wrote loyally to her sweetie back east. He promptly came west, married Lil, and launched prosperously into business with his new LIL ranch!

One rancher quarreled over possession of a bull with his long-time friend and shot him to death. So disgusted were cowboys on both sides of the argument that they roped the bull, made a steer of it, and in huge letters put this brand on its side: MURDER. Then they turned the animal loose and drove it off onto the open range, unwanted and unclaimed.

A short time later another man was slain — and the same steer was seen nearby. Then another. And another. The steer became a terrible omen, a harbinger of death. Any cowboy who saw it would fearfully drive it off lest it bring more tragedy. It became a pariah throughout the West. That happened half a century or more ago, and to this day, it is said, the MURDER steer still roams. Old-timers tell of seeing it by moonlight; young cowboys swear they have encountered it in the mists of dawn. It is talked about at many a campfire. And it is still feared.

In July, 1868, cowboy Jess Hitson was alone on a range when he found an unbranded calf. He lassoed the animal and built a fire nearby preparatory to branding it. Just then — *zing!* — an arrow knocked off his hat.

Jess dropped down behind the tied calf to shoot back at attacking Indians. All that afternoon his six-shooters held them off, but in the end the savages claimed another victim. No white man ever saw Jess Hitson again.

How do we know all that? Because three years later a full-grown steer was captured, and burned on its side was this:

### 7-4-68 INDIANS
### HOT AS HELL
### JH

Jess had used his red-hot running iron to burn his own obituary and had cut the calf loose to carry it away. It was in cowboy character, too, that Jess took time in the face of death to comment on the weather.

Peter Coffin branded his cows with the outline of a coffin holding a capital P inside it. Nobody could ever mistake his stock. A man named Mulkey burned MUL over the picture of a key for his brand, and a Mr. Starr uses a star. Ranchers from Essex, England, registered the SX brand, and others from Iowa honored their home state by burning their cows IOA. Innumerable square-and-compass brands are used by loyal Masons. And members of the Odd Fellows, Elks, Knights of Columbus, and other fraternities are loyal to their brethren when designing brands.

Brands grow first out of simple geometric designs — straight lines, squares, angles, circles, ovals, often with odd names. Straight lines become "bars" or "rails." A circle may be called a circle or an "oh." If it is flattened, it may become a "goose egg." If it joins other circles, they usually become "links." A square is called a "box." Infinite variety is found in the combinations of initials and numerals, but perhaps most interesting are the picture brands.

What would cause a rancher to choose a picture for his stamping iron? Nature? Surely, for there are countless lightning, tree, cloud, sunset, snake, and mountain brands. And the cowboy's everyday tools — ladders, camp kettles, stirrups, knives, guns — all are pictured on cows. The only requirement of a brand is that it be individual — unlike any other rancher's in your state or vicinity (registration laws govern this) — and that it be difficult for thieves to change by burning over. Remember the famous Oklahoma ranch 101? Thieves used to steal 101 cattle and reburn them Box O just by making a square of the two straightline 1's. Many others which proved too easy to alter have been changed.

Brands are not used only on cattle. A rancher is likely to brand everything he possesses — all his livestock, saddles, harness, wagons, cars, fences, windmills, doors, guns, stationery, and his name. He will become known as "Camp Kettle" Williams, or "Bar B Q" Campbell (a famous Texan), or "Circle 2" Jones. If in ten more years young Tom Reid is signing his checks " '45' Reid," there will be nothing unusual about it.

Nor does the branding stop with the ranchman. Curtains in Mrs. Rancher's home may have appliqued brands. Pillow slips and sheets need no ugly ink marks if the brand is proudly embroidered there. The guest book or photo album may be bound in thick tan leather with brands burned on, and the lamp shade may show the same set of "cow curlicues." House slippers are often branded, as are play suits and street dresses. The lapel ornament Mrs. Rancher wears to church and town is likely to be a set of silver stamping irons in miniature, two to three inches long. Western stores sell all these items and more.

Pie crusts are pricked with a fork not in simple geometric patterns or fancy floral designs but with the ranch brand; so, too, the brand design may appear on the icing of the Sunday cake. The son of the rancho likes to wear his dad's brand on practically every-thing, and he may even have it tattooed sailor-fashion on his skin. And the daughter — the slender, tanned, irresistible beauty who dances as well as she rides — is likely to startle her classmates at finishing school by coming to the pool in an elaborately branded bathing suit.

Flower gardens and hedgerows are often laid out to form the ranch brand. A nearby cliff face or a hillside may show the distinc-tive marking in colossal size, one such brand on a mountainside being 200 feet across and visible for many miles. Ranch apples, for the super-fancy trade, may be heat-treated by sunshine — colored in contrast by use of bits of tape at ripening time. Thousands of guests on ranches, as well as ranch folk themselves, burn the ranch brand on their own arms, calves, backs, or even faces by use of sunshine. (You can have fun doing this wherever you live.) You simply cut your design from adhesive tape, stick it on, and expose yourself to the sun for several hours. If you get a good tan, you will have a genuine brand that won't wash off.

A Mrs. Carlos Gonzales got her brand in a less healthful way. When she came to a New Mexico hospital for an operation, nurses were startled to find a five-inch brand scar burned on her flesh.

"Carlos, he brand me," said the Mexican woman simply, "so no other man can take. I am his. He brand his horses, cows, saddles, ever'teeng. Is good, no?"

Is good, yes! At least many have thought so, for thousands of women have been fire-branded, voluntarily or through force. But it's not a practice to be encouraged!

My Phoenix home is a picturesque Indian pueblo of sun-baked adobe bricks, and in the dining room hangs a chandelier that has been a conversation piece for years. It was made of five genuine branding irons, artfully forged into a circle by good friend Roby Goff, a college professor. This home has three Indian style fireplaces, and beside each are two or three genuine branding irons that have served admirably as pokers. They also delight guests, who enjoy heating the irons to a glowing red then burning their designs on pieces of pine-board kindling to take home. Many of these Arizona souvenirs now hang in dens in New York City, Detroit, Milwaukee, even in London and Paris. With each has gone a little of the Arizona legend.

Many men have made important collections of branding irons. I think of my old friend Ken T. Palmer, an attorney turned realtor, who after helping develop the renowned rich village of Scottsdale, Arizona, moved northward twenty miles and established an even more picturesque new town called Carefree. Ken's love of cowboying led him into wrought-iron work as a hobby, so he forged what is probably the world's largest branding iron. It is taller than a basketball player and weighs almost as much — too much for us cream-puff office cowpokes to lift. It leans against a red boulder beside his mansion in Carefree, and shows Pinnacle Peak, a mountain top not far away:

Ken has never burned that iron on the hide of a cow. But, said he, "I'm saving it for use when dinosaurs come back."

Ken and I and our families were vacationing together one summer in Santa Barbara, California. (Arizonans sometimes are just that disloyal!) We were poking up and down the old streets of that truly old Spanish town and came to a truly old man sitting in a truly old chair asleep in the sun in front of a truly old livery stable. A sign over the door dated the place — 1877. We didn't awaken that proprietor, but we poked on inside. Six horses, for modern dudes, were stabled there. But back in a far corner was a 10-foot-high pile of junk; old broken wheels, discarded harness, pure junk.

We poked into that. Lo, down under there we found a pile-up of more than 250 genuine cattle branding irons!

We awakened the fossil out front, dickered, rented a trailer and hauled all those irons to Phoenix. Ken displayed them for years, then sold them to Bud Brown, who put them in his dance barn north of Phoenix for latter-day dudes to enjoy.

But of all the branding iron collectors in America, none ever equaled my good friend John P. Hale, an insurance man at Mesa, Arizona. John went overboard. Everywhere he'd travel, coast to coast, he'd maneuver to beg, buy, or snitch irons from neighborhood ranches. He had so many hundreds of them in time that Mrs. Hale said either they went out of the house or she did. So he built a museum for them in his back yard. But in more time both John and his beloved wife passed on. The irons were sold to a Phoenix philanthropist, C. E. Van Ness, who gave them to the Phoenix Boy Scouts. They hang in the Scouts' Council building, a permanent exhibit rich with lore of the western range. John Hale and I had written a book on branding lore, *Hot Irons* (now out of print), which sold through eleven large editions. He was the authority; I simply did the writing. John often lectured on cattle brands, delighting his audiences.

"The many manifestations of the branding urge are amusing individually and significant as a whole," I once heard him tell a class at Arizona State University. "They add weight to the premise that a cattle brand is really an escutcheon of heraldry.

"The branding iron, in truth, is not just a tool for marking livestock. It is the scepter of a vast new saddled knighthood more glamorous and more honest than the chivalry of medieval Europe. In the meaning of brand symbols — their origin and the tradition and stories behind them — is the whole spirit and history of the cattle country and of the individuals who are keeping alive that history. It is a study in pure Americana, although most American scholars have as yet failed to approach the cowboy through his official coat of arms — the brand.

"I can think of no better way to show how brands figure in

westerners' hearts than to tell the story of my own experience. I was hunting deer in the Arizona ranch country when I came to an old abandoned schoolhouse. Buried in floor dust was the hardwood top of a desk such as children used years ago. In a city, it would have been carved with initials, aimless scrolls, comic faces, and such. But this one had been carved with a dozen or more ranch brands. There was the Flying H of Pecos McFadden, the Lazy Y 4 of the Kleinmans, the Double Circle, the Open A Cross, the Quarter Circle U, the Y Slash Z, and the Broken Arrow. Also there was the T Turkey Track with DOC under it. When I got back home, lugging the desk with me, I hunted up Doc Kline, now a man turning gray, and he almost cried when he saw that old desk where as a kid he had carved his daddy's brand.

"And so," John concluded, "it seems to me that when the symbolic force of a thing can dominate both work and play, it holds high significance. Branding is just that important in Arizona and all of Western America."

# XII.  HOW TO ENJOY THE RODEO

In spite of the fact that we live here in the cow country, most Arizonans rarely ever see a cow.  The guest from out of state is more likely to visit a cattle ranch than is the person born and reared in urban Phoenix.  But all of us — easterners and Arizonans alike — tend to think that "cowboy" and "rodeo" are synonymous.  And we aren't far wrong; the old workaday cowpoke dearly loves to stop work, gather with his buddies and have some rodeo fun.

There's no reason why we shouldn't join him.  Millions of Americans do pay to see rodeos each year, more than pay to see football games, and almost as many as see baseball.  Moreover, the whole story of rodeo is a long and intricate one which you are urged to study.  But if you are seeing one for the first time, or even if you are an old arena fan, you need some guidance toward getting the most enjoyment.  So let's start with a bit of background.

Rodeos probably were begun about 1870, for the express purpose of pleasure.  But we the people have never demanded enough audience participation to understand what's going on.  We realize that the cowboy is the most admired male who ever trod this earth, and we cheer when he bursts out of Chute No. 1 on a snorting, bucking, twisting bronco, spurring the brute and waving his hat grandly. We think of him as living in a utopia all his own.

What he is doing, however, isn't as soul-satisfying as it looks. Actually, he is showing off. In real life the cowboy doesn't ride many bucking horses. If he gets a horse that bucks, he promptly trains the bucking out of him; a cow horse is for *work,* not showoff. This could be said also of that horrendous sport called bulldogging, another act in the rodeo arena. In real life no cowboy is so stupid as to run out on a horse, leap from the saddle, grab a steer's horns and wrestle him to the ground in a dangerous flurry. No, most of the rodeo contests are pure circus, with very little relation to life on the open range.

There is one major exception — roping. So in my limited space here, then, I shall give you a bit of insight into the one phase of rodeo that is least understood and least appreciated, and you can know that at the same time you are absorbing some genuine lore of the cattle range. Ladee-e-e-ees and gennlemun (imitating the arena announcer) let me now present *the magnificent rodeo roper:*

Sooner or later every outdoor man comes to realize that, next to food and a woman, his most comforting possession is likely to be an ordinary piece of rope. There is no limit to what he can do with it. He starts with a bit of string pulling a toy, and by the time he is age five it's a 10-foot length of clothesline snitched from out back of the house. With this he enjoyably hangs himself from a tree limb, trips parents down steps, and binds a brother to a stake for Indian burning. By age seven he almost certainly has used it to lasso the dog and/or the annoying little girl next door. If he lives western, or lives eastern and looks at television (which includes just about all the males in North America) he grows up knowing that it is important thus to throw a loop and catch something. In his Walter Mitty moments the pent-up penthouse lad over Fifth Avenue — Lord help him — is able to gallop furiously across the sod, throw his long loop gracefully and bring down a 2,000-pound fire-snorting bull. By the time he is fifteen, the real-life lad on the ideal real-life ranch is able to do that in fact as well as fancy.

From this, over the decades, has sprung the most exacting, most artistic of all the rodeo contests. For those who can appreciate the subtler nuances of it, roping will dominate the show in Phoenix, Tucson, Scottsdale, Payson, Prescott, wherever else in our state and elsewhere the cow folk gather for recreation.

Brawn and guts and reasonable practice on Sunday afternoons may make you a competent bronc buster or steer wrestler. But roping — now there's a sport of such delicate shadings, such exacting technique, that talent at it sets any man apart. The roper cannot get by with mediocrity. His performance is like violin music, it's either superb or it's lousy, the critter is either caught or it isn't. This does not mean that the roper is permitted to be a pampered prima donna; or in the democracy of the corrals is regarded any more highly than is the manure scooper. It does mean that every able-bodied male — and female — who is exposed to any sort of ranch and rodeo life is sure to spend considerable time rehearsing with a rope.

Thus the rope itself and other factors contributing to the roper's skill are given the most careful consideration.

\* \* \*

Now there are ropes and ropes. The first one, we can reasonably assume, was a short length braided of flexible vegetable fibres by Mr. *Pithecanthropus Erectus* sitting in his cave home $x$ thousand years B. C. We still braid them of flexible vegetable fibres, sitting in cavelike factories in Massachusetts, which is the cordage center of the nation. Since 1824 the Plymouth Cordage Company, notably, has made ropes for those he-men brothers of the cowboys, the sailors, who — for some unaccountable reason — call all ropes "lines." That firm still dominates the rope field.

During the latter part of the nineteenth century the Plymouth people specialized in a fine quality "Yacht Rope" made of the highest grade fibres, a creamy white with a silken sheen, tougher than any other. These came from the center of the best abaca (manila) herbs grown in the Philippines, and the boys who roped the wind into their sails loved it.

But not until 1905 did a Plymouth drummer happen to show his fancy "line" to some cow people out West. He was in Dallas, at Padgitt Brothers saddlery. One of the Padgitts had cowboys experiment with it, and orders followed at once. The Yacht Rope, soft and easy to handle yet very strong, seemed a natural for tossing at the head of a cow. It replaced the conventional lariat rope that Plymouth had begun advertising in 1895. But according to Professor Clifford P. Westermeier in his distinguished work *Man, Beast Dust,* it was not until 1916 that the Yacht Rope was first introduced into rodeo. It was brought in by Colonel Jim Eskew of the Spark Show.

Half a century later that type of rope still holds first place in contestants' favor, though many riders have individual ideas of what kind to buy. A few make their own. Some cowpokes think that a rope hand-woven from the fibres of mescal — that strange, beautiful "century plant" flower of the Southwest from which comes human food, cattle food, sewing thread and three kinds of drinking liquor including the fiery *tequila* — is the very best of all. Other men, gifted with unique skill and patience, have made wonderfully good ropes from rawhide.

"You can make yours of red Christmas ribbon if it'll get the job done," cowboy Hal Moore told us succinctly, one day in Phoenix.

He was gibing at some pals who had worked up an argument about ropes. They gibed back, and one thing led to another until, of course, they had a bet on. Ed Dubois bet Hal fifty bucks he couldn't make a ribbon rope that would lasso and hold a yearling. Hal got mad, got the ribbon, got to weaving, got on his horse, got his calf and got his money. It took two weeks, but so what? A deep principle was involved, wasn't there?

Size of rope is measured by its thread count. The typical lariat has eleven threads in each of three twisted strands, hence is called

33 count. Some are 30, some 36. This still means a rope smaller than a man's little finger — a fact which astounds dudes. It is incredibly strong, and its secret lies in its tight twisting. That's where Hal Moore won; he had to twist-braid $86 worth of red ribbons to win a $50 bet, but his honor — call it that — was saved.

Well then, the roper acquires his rope. He usually calls it that — "rope" — but he may use the term "lariat" which is more precisely correct. It in turn stems from the Spanish-Mexican term *la reata,* meaning (surprise!) the rope. He won't likely say "lah'-ree-at" in proper Bostonian, he'll say "lairt" in proper Tucsonian. So "Gimme my lairt rope" is correct Arizona idiom.

He treasures the thing. He doesn't like to lend it, nor let it get too wet or too dry or too dirty. He carries it from rodeo to rodeo in a special tin can, or at least in a canvas bag. Cudd Jenkins was so forgetful he left his suitcase and his wife in Phoenix when the rodeo was over and had to drive back from Casa Grande to get them, but his canned lariat was in the front seat beside him. Mrs. Jenkins did not get mad; she understood.

Any cowboy likes to condition his rope. Often he ties one end to his saddle horn and drags the rest of it loose on the ground for days. This is not as silly as it sounds. Most new-bought rope comes stiff, like wire. Dragging it that way "supples" it; makes it not dishrag limp but softly responsive, just right for coiling, looping, and throwing.

Lovingly he curls one end into a sort of eyehole and braids (sailors would call this "splices") the end back onto itself. Usually he tightens this around a light metal oval the size of an egg, a thing called a hondo (or honda; from the Spanish) which enables the other end of the rope to slip through it easily. He knots that other end, or splices it back onto itself to prevent fraying and permit easy emergency slip-through.

"How long is a cowboy lariat?" somebody asked a high school class in one of those goofy tests. This was in Arizona, too, not New England. Only six per cent came anywhere near correct. Some said fifty yards, some said a hundred yards.

133

You can't blame the kids; most folk aren't length conscious. The Hickok Belt manufacturers commissioned a fine artist named Leigh to paint a picture of a roper in action. He ought to have known better, for he was at "home on the range," but Mr. Leigh gave his roper about fifty feet of loop and stretch-out *plus* a coil in his left hand which would have reached from here to the courthouse.

Usually a lariat is only twenty to twenty-five feet long. Until recent years it was twenty-five to thirty feet, but as horses got faster the long rope became cumbersome, the throw and catch easier with the shorter one. The roper needs that short length for a quick, sure stab at the animal.

Incidentally, a real artist with a rope can do many things besides lasso with it. He is darn near as versatile as was the kid with the piece of clothesline. He can flip a rattlesnake off a rock, snatch a pretty girl's hair ribbon, or even whip-kill a man who is trying to shoot him. Many such instances are on record.

\* \* \*

The rodeo roping act itself is so short and swift that few spectators really appreciate its artistry. There are set rules for it, the organized (Rodeo Cowboys Association) contestants abide by them or lose any chance for prize money. But the old whanghides who on holidays just rope for fun and maybe a little side betting, may have variations in the rules to suit their fancy.

The RCA sport goes like this:

A calf is ejected from its chute into the open arena. Scared, it travels fast. Waiting in a pen or "box" behind a triggered rope is a mounted rider carrying *two* lariats, one in hand, one on his saddle. When the calf has passed a given line thirty feet out — and not before, lest he be disqualified — the rider spurs. His horse shoots out in pursuit. The rider is already swinging his loop. At proper range he throws and (he hopes) catches.

In the same coordinated motion, the horse skids to a stop and *backs up* thus holding taut the rope, which is "dallied"\* to the saddle horn, while the man leaps off, grabs the tight rope, runs down it, grabs the struggling calf, throws it, and ties any three feet together with a piggin' string. Finished, he throws both hands high, thus signaling the timers, who stop their watches. All ropers compete not only against an animal weighing five to ten times what they weigh, but against dirt, danger, and time.

How much time is the roper allowed?

Not how much, but how *little!* Some sweet dude asked Will Rogers how much and he said, "Not long enough to do much knittin', Ma'am." In other words, about the time you'd take to read this paragraph.

And that means from the instant the cowboy gets the "Go!" until the moment he throws up his hands to signal "tied." The world's record calf roping at this writing is eight seconds. It is unofficial. There is no official record and never can be, the RCA tells us, because of varying conditions. But times are recorded.

Of course, you don't have to break a record to win money. But you do need speed and great skill. If your first throw misses you try with your other rope — while the seconds tick off the clock. The calf may not cooperate; it may jump around and buck and bawl, thus entertaining the folks in the bleachers while your prize money wastes away. If your horse decides to stop dead in its flight and thus "bust" the calf down with the taut rope, you can be penalized ten seconds; you must throw the calf yourself. Moreover, the confounded calf may not run in a straight line in the first place, but may side-step and weave and turn so that you miss both loop throws and have to slink back wondering why you don't take up some profitable sport like bank robbin'.

Or, if you do catch him and tie his feet, the calf may kick out of the piggin' string just before the judges inspect him and pronounce your tie a good one. That tie is usually a quick double wrap and a double half-hitch. The piggin' string is simply a short, small rope

---

*"Dally" a rope is from the Spanish *de la vuelta,* meaning to give another turn or two, usually with a clinching half-hitch, around the saddle horn.

carried in your mouth or under your belt for quick access. It's the type farmers might use to tie a pig.

Techniques, and rules, of course vary in the other roping events. Because a steer may be four times as heavy as a calf, the throw and tie usually are accomplished by two men in an event called team roping. One loops over the head, the other ropes a hind foot. Thus the skills vary. If there are horns it's one thing, if the critter's a muley it's another. If the arena is hard and dry the speed is stepped up. But dust can blind you. And if, as often happens, the arena is so wet that the animal sinks knee-deep in mud at each plunge, just *try* to rope a hind foot! Yet the boys do so. It's a matter of precision timing all the way; and of almost unbelievable skill.

"A piece of hemp in the hands of a good roper becomes a thing alive," says Lex Connelly, head wrangler of the Rodeo Cowboys Association. "He can make it go out in a flat loop with an angle from right to left, staying on a plane to catch the two horns of a running steer. He can make the loop hit the ground and roll hooplike to catch the two hind feet of a steer. He can aim and angle his loop so that it ropes a calf turning right or left; or throw with a sort of roundabout scooping motion that will catch the calf ducking and diving in front of him."

This artistry came directly from the work of the old-time cowboy. In the pioneering days there were no fences; the rope was the only way to secure an animal for branding, dehorning, and doctoring. Generally, only steers were roped, for only steers were shipped. Calves were rounded up and branded in an entirely different manner; they were held together in the herd with their mothers so that the riders could work quietly in, heel a calf and drag it to the branding fire. But the steer roper — *wham!* He'd race jet-propelled across the prairie and rope his animal in a flash of exciting, exacting and dangerous movie-and-TV action, long before movies and TV were even dreamed of. It was the only way.

Thus in the birthdays of rodeo, steer roping alone was dominant, calf roping nonexistent. Arizona tradition says that the first public rodeo roping for fun and prizes was held at Prescott, probably in the 1880's. The boys held a herd of steers there by the courthouse, turned them loose one at a time as a roper dashed out to do his stuff while spectators cheered from the sidewalks. This was so much fun for all concerned (except the steers) that the sport spread fast over the great cattle state. But it was also, obviously, very rough. The steer would flop over or somersault hard, grunt loud enough to be heard in Phoenix, and lie there stunned. Often its bones were broken, its hide torn. Down in Texas the legislature even passed a law saying that steers could not be roped and thrown from horseback, except for the purpose of branding.

The pioneers couldn't afford to cripple their steers, yet they didn't turn to calves at first; they substituted — of all things — goats. For years goat roping was popular in Texas, Kansas, Oklahoma, New Mexico, and Arizona, though not on the West Coast. By the early 1900's calf roping had supplanted fun with the goats. Also, fewer steers were being roped because the Society for the Prevention of Cruelty to Animals had become quite active. The SPCA still takes a dim view of all rodeo contests; with, it must be confessed, at least some crumb of justification.

Here in mid-century, roping is the most popular participant event in rodeo. It is a basic thing, a fundamental and picturesque part of cowboy work. Besides which, it is fun. Thousands of Americans rope just for the pleasure of it. It doesn't "sore them up," is not expensive to try, is recreational. But money-making perfection at it demands a monotony of practice, a high-level devotion which weeds out all but a few. Steer roping has dwindled to a small group of highly specialized men who dominate all contests. Calf roping is the bright goal which lures young men by the hundreds.

* * *

Not one of them in either category can get to first base — if you'll permit a figure from another sport — without a horse that is smarter than the man.

137

Much is made of the cutting horse, the polo pony, the show animal everywhere. But by contrast they are mere puppets against that specialist of the rodeo arena, the roper's horse. The roper must *know;* must think, if ever a horse can, and do so with split-second precision. In polo, in cutting work, in reining contests, the man is astride his horse at all times. Even in steer wrestling, when you leave your horse his work is done. But in roping you have to depend on him while you are afoot going down the rope and tying the calf.

Thus the matter of horses is the greatest worry that a roper has. He can develop some fine prospects and think that everything is just right, then start on the rodeo circuit and after three or four shows the animals will completely quit him. Perhaps it's because the things that a roping horse is called on to do are not natural. Getting back on a rope, pulling it to keep it tight at all times, is "unreasonable" to him, and as Lex Connelly says, "Many hosses will take advantage of the opportunity not to do it."

The horse has to "score" well. That is, he must stay behind the barrier, then get out of that box at full speed at just the right instant. This means he can't rear, can't turn, sulk or freeze up, can't be nervous, can't do anything but just squat for that sudden dart out after the calf or steer. Horses are as different as people, hence as unpredictable.

When he does dart out, everything your horse does must be done automatically. You are busy with the ropes, you can't cue him much, so he is on his own. He mustn't run too close to the calf nor lay back too far, else you can't make your catch. Then he mustn't keep the rope too loose nor too tight, mustn't jump around nor relax nor do anything else natural, mustn't even show love for his master as did pretty black Toro in a show at Tucson. In the leap-off, Toro's owner lost his hat in the mud and manure. Toro saw it, forgot his rope, walked over and picked up the hat and gently delivered it to his master — while the spectators applauded and the cowboy lost $1,000 prize money.

138

Wherefore, it is not surprising that some cowboys have paid $5,000 or more for a good roping horse. We could list dozens of great ones. Old-timers speak of Baldy, for instance. He was developed by Ike Rude in the 1930's, and sold in 1942 to Clyde Burke for a then record sum of $2,500. People said Baldy could do everything but bake a cake, and was more dependable than your mother.

Such animals undoubtedly go to horse heaven, the cowpokes feel. They also feel that, the Lord willin', it would be a happy place for themselves to go in the hereafter.

# XIII.   YOUR HOME ON THE RANGE

One invariable and understandable reaction of persons coming to Arizona from less colorful regions is their urge to rub elbows with some genuine cow folk, to get outdoors and see for themselves if ranching is as romantic as the storytellers make it seem. From this has arisen a uniquely American enterprise, the guest ranch industry; we have provided you the opportunity not only to visit a ranch, but actually to live there for as long as you wish. The man who started this in Arizona was Charles Poston; thank him for providing your home on the range.

Nobody could possibly have guessed what a precedent Charlie was establishing when he rode into the southwestern sun country a century ago. He was the first important tourist in this region, the first of millions who have come not expecting to be entertained but to create their own entertainment, seeking only the proper setting and atmosphere. He found it in the ranch-country village of Tubac, Arizona, in what was then a truly wild and open land.

"Never dreamed of such a charming country!" he said on arrival — there's written record of it. "I'm a lawyer out of Washington, D. C., and let me tell you this — people back there'd give anything just to spend one month out here."

141

There was no way of bringing many tourists out in 1854, but Charlie did what many another traveler has since done — took root. Forthwith he announced that he was *alcalde* of Tubac. This meant simply that he was the town's mayor, father-confessor, chief counselor, head man. Since there was no other elected or appointed authority around, he made it stick. What the *alcalde* did there is priceless, and his own handwritten record has become indelible in the lore of our region:

"There was no priest nearer than Altar . . . Though self-appointed head of the civil government, I proceeded to exercise magisterial functions and formally wedded all couples who presented themselves. This proceeding became popular, for I charged no fee and gave each bride a five-dollar dot. So all was merry, and among the dozens of almost naked urchins that played on the thoroughfares of the little pueblo, many had been named or re-named in honor of me.

"Later there came the reaction. I had intruded my American ideas into Mexican customs and had to stand the consequences. I was met with scowls and curses instead of smiles. A priest had arrived, learned of the matrimonial peculiarities of the town and immediately had excommunicated the whole bunch from the church. The women particularly were wild.

"I squared it, though it cost me about five hundred dollars. I had the priest re-marry them and topped it all with a holiday and a grand *baile* (dance festival) in honor of the happy brides and grooms, not excluding their children."

Such an imaginative, honorable, and good-humored man deserves all the credit we can give him. Charlie moved back east, but couldn't stand it back there whenever he thought of Arizona, so he'd come back here "for a spell of rest on the front porch of a ranch house somewhere." Thus he was the first steady customer of the ranch folk, even though nobody thought of him as such. Finally he gave up traveling and just stayed, adopting the strange, dangerous, beautiful region for his own. The sunshine, so rare in Washington,

142

was a beneficent glory out here. The natives showed an easy hospitality, a live-and-help-live attitude in sharp contrast to the dog-eat-dog pattern elsewhere. Probably he wasn't consciously romantic — few truly romantic persons are — but he perceived that this region was for living and loving and getting the most out of life.

Decades had to pass, however, before we had the insight to capitalize on Charlie's precedent. We were too busy raising cattle, which is hot hard work, so that we damned the sunshine rather than praised it, and when any of you touring easterners showed up you got in our hair. We bow-legged, leather-faced sons of the sun started calling you "dudes" and for at least sixty years applied it as a term of derision. You didn't look like one of us because you were pasty faced and you wore strange city clothes and had what we felt were prissy manners and mannerisms and spoke a strange version of the American language — you'd say "bawth" and "hahlf-pahst two" and "indubitably" (and we wondered what in the high hoppin' hades that meant!), and if you meant over yonder you'd say "ovah theah." So naturally we figured you were an inferior clan.

But in the fullness of time we faced some depressions. The dollar became hard to collect, the mortgage came due, our best bull died, and America generally was at low financial ebb. Then one day you and a few of your snobbish companions rode right up to our ranch-house door. You were horrible looking — dudes to the gills — but night was settling down and we lived a long way from the next ranch and the inviolable law of hospitality made us bid you a hearty welcome. You therefore washed up at our well, ate at our table, and slept in our beds. Next day, relaxed and smiling, you seemed a mite more human, so we invited you to take a saddle horse and ride out and admire our stock. Every rancher wants his stock admired, just as every artist wants his pictures praised, every girl her figure, every farmer his potatoes, every author his books. You did admire the cows, and our scenery as well; we hadn't thought much about the scenery, but durn if it wasn't right purty, no foolin'. You stayed all that day and another night, you patted our little children and our

143

dogs on the head, you praised our wives' pies, and you said yes the government ought to do something to get rid of these murderous raiding Indians. Then next morning as you started to leave, you felt that you had imposed on good ranch hosts unbearably, so you offered a twenty-dollar bill.

"No no, Sir. No." The bankrupt rancher rumbled, fierce of eye. "Decent strangers are welcome in my home long as I have beans to boil and jerky on the rafters."

But you, gentlefolk that you were, had observed the signs of depression and despair in these hard times, so you left that $20 on the dresser carefully weighed down. Next day your host and hostess found it, and reacted as normal beings should; they took the money and bought groceries with it.

Precisely where that apocryphal but momentous event occurred I haven't the faintest idea, and the origin of dude ranching doesn't really matter. The point is, we southwestern cattle ranchers in time of need did begin accepting strangers for pay, especially in sun-parched Arizona. Several years had to pass, however, before our relations with you were entirely cordial. Soon after you discovered you had to pay a little for accommodations, you became demanding, you weren't satisfied with our rustic homes. With a billion-dollar view over a million sun-tinted acres, you complained because the toilet was twenty-five yards away. So we put in plumbing, for which you paid again and again. You wanted fresh sheets every week and a saddle with a cushioned seat and liquor before supper and music after supper and mail every day. Where you first paid $25 a month, you began paying $25 a week, thence onward and upward to a modern $75 or $100 a *day!* Oddly enough, you liked that — a fact we sensible Arizonans have never understood; apparently you thought you were getting something big if you paid a big price for it. So we began straining ourselves to supply every conceivable service and luxury, even though it has meant getting far, far indeed from the true working-ranch life.

144

Romance had to be developed for you; romance as you had preconceived it. You lacked the sensitivity for our eternal verities, our things of the spirit. You had to have Hollywood cowboys strumming guitars, cowboys who wore cerise shirts and crooned about the Arizona moo-moo-moo-moo-oo-ooooon. Your sisters — and sometimes your immoral wives — married the crooners, then discovered they were unromantic except for pay. You wanted this sham glamor and you got it, and all of us were shamed.

Fortunately both we and you in time began to recognize that buffoonery, so that now at long last the serious business of guest ranching in Arizona (and throughout the West) is getting onto a sound basis. Easterners are not as snobbish or naive as they once were, westerners are not as avaricious. You have made it clear that we have something you want, and we now supply it in the same ethical business way that we sell our steers. You have stopped calling us yokels; we have stopped calling you dudes. You know and we know that the cerise-shirted cowboy is a phony and he himself admits it, grinning cordially and inviting you to join in singing "Home On The Range." We have mutual respect, and that's always a prelude to cordial personal and business relations. In short, the guest ranching industry has come of age.

The sunshine remains as our Number 1 drawing card, our primary attraction. Back in Bangor or Buffalo you read of a golf tournament in February, so you head for Phoenix. Or you look with horror at your doctor bills — $300 for sinus treatments or arthritis or pleurisy or anemia or whatever — plus the cost of drugs, and still you are no better; then you hear that the only person who ever dies in Arizona is the undertaker, and he starves to death. You look up the government records and see that sure enough Arizona does have abiding winter warmth and sun. You are fed up with overcoats and galoshes and you still have months to go, so you call to mama and say, "Honey, how about us going down to the Southwest for a little winter vacation?" Honey likes the idea, you can bet on that, and so next day you take a plane.

Under our sun, you seek restoration of mind and body, and likely enough you'll find it on one of our ranches. Planes and cars being what they are, you'll have moved fast, so that only forty-eight hours have elapsed since you were fighting snowdrifts, yet here you are perched on an Arizona corral fence at 10 A.M. listening to some picturesque (carefully trained) old cowpoke reciting po'try from maybe the pen of Don Rognon —

> Saddle strings
> Insignificant things —
> Just strips of oiled deerhide:
> But their pull is strong
> And their hold is long
> On the years when you used to ride.
>
> Saddle strings!
> An old heart sings
> Of days when the West was wide,
> And sighs. Perhaps
> To those saddle flaps
> A bit of his heart is tied.

Now that's nice sentiment, and you respond to it; it's all a far cry from The Office, the harassments back yonder in the eastern cold. Then maybe before you realize it the old pro there beside the fence has got you and your dude companions singing that prime ballad "A Cowboy's Life," written by Miss Verona Burkhard. Note the gay and galloping swing to it.

> The bawl of a steer to a cowboy's ear
> Is music of sweetest strain;
> And the yelping notes of the gray coyotes
> To him are a glad refrain.

146

For a kingly crown in a noisy town
His saddle he wouldn't change;
No life so free as the life we see
Way out on the open range.

There are more stanzas to it, and you gradually learn them as the hours leisurely pass. Before you realize it you are becoming part of the West, part of Arizona under the sun.

The individual setting of our ranches often was too crudely rural for entertainment. So, our ranch owners have dressed their spreads. Houses now are made picturesque, but in traditional ranch style. Fences are stained logs, rustic signs swing on rawhide, trees are trimmed, manure piles are hauled away, fancier clothing is worn, and people bathe. Both the rancher and the cowboys he hires are career men, not so much in roping and dehorning and branding and castrating, but in the higher paid profession of showmanship. They are workers with professional pride, codes of ethics, assurance and poise. You recognize this, so you come westward without fear of disillusionment.

Now, how can you individually get the most out of your Arizona ranch vacation, how can you share in this cattle-land romance? In short, "Where shall I go?" or, speaking for friends, "What place shall I recommend?"

You face one first decision — high country or low? If it's winter you'd best stick to our valleys, although some ranches in the wooded hills can do well by you all year. If it's summer you'd best go on up there where the coolness and the rainbow trout are. High altitudes are cool all summer, and less dry, so you'll enjoy heavier verdure, a vast green wilderness rich with history. Around Phoenix and Tucson, anywhere under 3,000 feet altitude, moisture is almost nonexistent except for irrigation, but you'll be enriched by a winter warmth and a colorful desert life. This fact has spawned a surprising number of resort hotels and surburban ranches as well as genuine dude spots farther out. Wickenburg, Arizona, claims to be the dude

147

ranch capital of the world, with some justification, yet it has no great advantage over many another semi-desert area. Do make your inquiries well in advance; read travel magazines, send out here for chamber of commerce literature, get the facts and the reservations before you come.

No matter which ranch you choose, go there determined to court relaxation. Do *not* order your business mail forwarded. Let your stock broker wonder where you have gone. Relaxation comes easily and delightfully if you allow it. You'll rest a few days or hours then find your bodily batteries re-charged, so that you'll want to be up and doing again — but in a different sphere. Rodeos, square dances, horse shows, hunting lost mines, cookouts in the hills, rock hounding, all these and more will be on your ranch agenda, take it or leave it *ad lib*.

One more worry confronts every newcomer to the western guest ranch — "What shall I wear?" Indeed, "What shall I wear now that I plan to live permanently in Arizona?" These questions we hear each day.

Yours is a natural and logical interest, and don't let the matter of clothing disturb you. Just go easy, and wait. Prices in Arizona are no higher than they are back east, often are lower, and many of the things you might bring are likely to be wrong for this area. When you cross the Mississippi River coming westward, styles change. Oh we are "dressy" — heavens yes! Finest fashion shows in America probably are those staged on the terrace beside the pools in our lavish resorts, and many of our urban costumes are right out of the world's swankiest designers' salons. But generally, our costumes are "western" in some hint or subtle touch; sometimes not so subtle.

To the uninitiated, "Westerners will wear anything so long as it's made of leather." We do like hide of deer and cow. We'll all wear a suede jacket, given the chance. But we aren't yokels in rough hair-on stuff. Truth is, the heavy emphasis on "western" clothing that held during the 1940's and 50's has edged off, and Arizonans now wear modish new types of outfits, fewer of the famous old Levi blue

148

denims, fewer fringed jackets and frontier pants. We reserve those for rodeo week and outdoor events. Exception will be the ranches, where almost anything western still goes.

Your objective, then, will be to bring out a limited supply of what you have, study the styles in your new environment, and buy your new outfit right here. Then you'll be stylish, with no extra cost. This may help you find that sun-country serenity which we all court.

# XIV.  RARE, MEDIUM, OR WELL DONE

The setting for this delightful adventure is anywhere under the sun; under the aspens along the Coronado Trail; near the junipers of the northern plateaus; beside the sahuaros of the border zones. Build up a little rectangle of rocks about one by two feet by six inches high, or if no rocks are available, dig a hole. Inside, make a fire. Use pine for kindling only; burn oak, ash, mesquite, ironwood, hickory, walnut, any dry hardwood. Start your fire thirty to sixty minutes ahead of supper time. Burn it down until the flame stops and you have two inches or so of ashes and glowing coals. Spread these evenly. Put a grill on top — the best I have ever found is a shelf out of an old refrigerator. It shouldn't rest more than four inches from the very hot coals. Put on T-bone steaks, one inch thick, and unseasoned.

Now sit back on your heels, cowboy fashion. You will receive no end of free advice from the company. Ignore it. Keep a long fork handy, also big salt and pepper shakers. As the drip forms a flame, move the meat. The fragrance will be maddening, and people will gather closer and closer. Watch the steak; when the under side is thoroughly brown, with a hint of charring along the bone, turn it. Now salt the cooked side heavily, and pepper sparingly. Never salt raw steak for broiling or you will lose the sweet juices; wait until the outside is seared. Order mama (or somebody whom you *can* order) to get busy with the other fixin's, because you're near ready. The rolls should be heated — they can be toasted along the edges of the grill while the meat sizzles — and everybody should already have been served with salad, vegetables, drink. Turn the T-bones once more and season on that side up. Signal that you're ready. You, and your guests, will know what to do from here.

The ritual is presented here in simplified form because anything that simplifies outdoor eating is desirable. You can, to be sure, flaunt your wealth; you can hire expensive chefs, buy elaborate equipment, and stage your picnic deluxe *ad lib*. You will end up spending ten times as much money for one-tenth as much fun. It is somehow essential to good picnics that the host personally do the main cooking; this presumably has more to do with proper dramatics than with gastronomics.

The "Steak Fry," then, is basic Arizonan, and the degree to which you perfect it is the measure of your adaptability in the land of the sun. Each man or woman, naturally, will develop his own techniques. I know one chap who covers his glowing coals with the green foliage of greasewood, then puts the raw meat right on top of that, without a grill. I was as doubtful as you, the first time, but his steaks were delicious. Many cooks, male especially, love to baste the steaks with various "secret" concoctions that are thick like gruel, and usually red. I'm ag'in that, on the premise that a lot of fancy seasoning conflicts with the most delectable flavor man knows — the *natural* flavor of fresh T-bone. But there is no law about this.

Barbecue is the result of smoke, and time. "Broil" and "barbecue" are not synonymous verbs; nothing is barbecued just because it was cooked over an open fire. And you will want to know both techniques of outdoor cooking.

The basic flavor which distinguishes true barbecue is that of hardwood smoke, preferably hickory. Never use pine or any other soft wood except for kindling. Somewhat more elaborate equipment is necessary for true barbecue; your fireplace must be deeper so as to accommodate a bigger bed of coals, and allow for a slow burning of logs at one end. There must be some kind of top over the meat to keep the smoke thick around it. This sounds crude. It is. But it also is effective, as tested now over the centuries. Almost any old pan, or whatever metal is available, will do for your cover. But don't plan on fifteen-minute cooking, and don't plan on serving steaks. Steaks were not meant for barbecuing, but for broiling. Best get other cuts of beef with suet mixed in, and cook them in rather large hunks. Then build the fire hours in advance, and allow from three to six hours (depending on the size of your cuts) for the slow and lazy cooking.

In the great barbecues for which Arizona is famous, pits are dug three to four feet deep and meat is put on the grill in hunks of fifty to a hundred pounds. Such grills usually are heavy hog fence netting spread on iron bars that cross the pit, and covers are sheets of metal roofing. The cooks wield pitchforks, rather than kitchen forks, for turning the meat. After two hours of it the cooks look like devils, for the smoke blackens them along with the beef.

Now, about sop. Some people call it soption. Some even call it sauce. But sauce is usually atrocious stuff you pour on *after* cooking. True barbecue sop need be nothing more potent and secret than salt, black pepper, and butter, intended primarily to keep the meat from drying out. (Bacon grease and suet can replace the butter.) Sop is daubed on the cooking meat every few minutes with a paint brush, or with a rag tied to a stick. Cooks at the really big barbecues use tubs of sop and apply it with new brooms.

There are, however, specialized "barbecue sauces" which can be used as cooking sop. These are likely to abound in chili pepper powder. Mind you, they aren't bad. Many a good soul will die and go to heaven never having tasted any barbecue sauce save this. I have even cooked hot barbecue personally, knowing that some guest

153

preferred it; when guests differ in their desires, chili can be in the sop for some of the meat, and only our salt-pepper-and-butter, for the rest.

Precise recipes for barbecue sop, indeed, are as varied as are human temperaments. As you experiment, you will gradually evolve your own idea of sop perfection.

Of the other meats, and of the other ways for cooking beef itself, there is no end of discussion. We analyze, explain, debate, demonstrate, remonstrate, share, and enjoy. One school of us holds that the butchered beef (or lamb, hog, deer, elk, javelina, antelope, quail, duck, or whatever) should be hung and chilled for a time to be properly aged for cooking. Others argue that the life heat can fuse right into the heat of the cooking fire, for best nourishment and flavor. Detailed instructions are offered for cooking camp son-of-a-gun out of sweetbreads and kidneys. The exact way to drop dumplings into a meat stew is more important to many open-air chefs than the politics of the next President. Most of us cut onions into every cooking pan that has meat in it, while others — obviously more refined — hold that we will never be civilized until we rid ourselves of war and onions.

You will learn by doing. There are no hard and fast recipes. There is basic common sense: you put raw meat somehow into proximity with fire, and you season it to taste, after which you can hardly starve. Nevertheless, our decades of talk about cooking have evolved some favorite procedures.

The fresh meats are first, but there are other items in our outdoor cuisine which must be considered at least briefly. Have you for instance, ever tried jerky? Our pioneers found deep-freeze units rather scarce on the southwestern desert, but they managed to preserve the surplusage of venison they acquired. They cut it into strips the size of your fingers and about six inches long, then hung it on wires in the open. After a day or two in our intensely dry air and hot sun, the meat had turned to stone, or a reasonable facsimile

154

thereof. No flies could blow it, any more than they could blow roast baking in an oven. No germ, I am sure, could survive on it. The pioneers gathered this jerked meat and hung it on the rafters of their homes for rainy-day consumption months or even years later.

You chew jerky as you work, if you are busy. You carry it in your saddlebags on roundup, or riding fence far from the home ranch. You put in a few handfuls for emergency on a long hunt. Or you just store it for family food when isolation or poverty makes fresher meat uncommon. Jerky is most palatable, possibly, when ground or pounded into a powder and cooked with flour or dumplings into a sort of stew. It can be made of any red meat — venison, buffalo, beef, and even horse or burro. In your exploration of the Southwest, therefore, put down jerky as one item to be sampled, and respected, for sure.

Citrus fruits have affected our southwestern way of life. Arizona's great oasis, the Valley of the Sun, wears the emerald green of orange and grapefruit groves. The orange tree is symbolic of warmth and sunshine; the chambers of commerce have exploited it unmercifully, and truly no other fruit has ever struck the American consciousness with the impact of the orange. Almost every home in the citrus regions uses orange, grapefruit, lemon, lime, tangerine, mandarin, and kumquat trees for landscaping. Our streets often are lined with them, as are our school yards and our courthouse lawns.

It is inevitable, then, that citrus fruits should have marked influence on our Arizona diet. In northern cities it is considered proper to serve half an orange with a spoon as a breakfast fruit. Pullman chefs slice a whole orange for you and serve it daintily on a plate, or squeeze it in a pretty little glass buried in a large bowl of ice. That's nice, but out here it sounds a bit silly; we practically bathe in orange juice. We seldom serve less than a pint to a person in our homes. We eat two or three oranges at a time, or we eat at least one whole grapefruit at a time; we mix the sections in salads, or in desserts; citrus punch, served afternoons and evenings, is a special delight. One result of all this, in addition to pleasure, is of course health. The cookbooks will guide you among the hundreds of citrus recipes. But one pet recipe I must squeeze in:

> ½ cup of lemon juice
> 1½ cups of sugar
> 1 quart of whole milk

Mix the lemon juice and sugar, and chill. Into this syrup pour the milk slowly, ice cold (to prevent curdling), beating rapidly with an egg beater. Freeze at once, with the kind of ice cream freezer you have to turn by hand. Let your mixture set hard. Serve plain, or garnish with mint, strawberry, blackberry, or what-have-you. This is "Sun-Country Sherbet" and absolutely perfect after a heavy dinner, or when you have a group in.

## Mexican Food

You must decide, when among us, whether you really like tamales or just like the idea. In short, are you a "Mexican food" addict, or aren't you?

When you come to Sante Fe, Albuquerque, San Antonio, El Paso, Tucson, Phoenix, San Diego, anywhere in our border land, any town big or small, inquire for Mexican restaurants. There's no need for you to seek out those restaurants which cater only to the tourist, providing his unaccustomed tongue with watered-down, "harmless" imitations. Rather, ask directions to the best Mexican food in town, as if you were an addict already, and a stranger only in this one city. But — take a friend, or confess your inexperience to the chef. Take their advice; start with something only moderately hot, say two tacos, and work your way on carefully from there. You may, indeed, become a fanatic for Mexican dishes, as many of us permanent residents are.

You may want to prepare your own Mexican foods. To encourage you, it is a pleasure herewith to recommend *Mexican Cookbook,* a small volume by Erna Fergusson. This has become a standard guide for the enthusiasts. Miss Fergusson stresses that chili and beans are only the beginning; that crude hot food, which used to pass as authentic, lacks the subtlety of flavor characteristic of real Mexican cookery. She omits those bizarre dishes which require you to import some extract from Peru, and simplifies matters so that all your ingredients can come from the corner grocery or, better, from any of many special supply stores in our towns. In such stores, moreover, you will learn that in our enthusiasm for savor, we have not limited ourselves to dishes of the Americas. We have freed our palates of their conventions; and if you will watch, you may see our housewives buying, matter of factly, herbs, oils, and spices clearly intended for some new adventure in cookery.

# XV.  OASIS

Whenever Arizona is mentioned, the word "Phoenix" usually
follows close by. That's understandable; Phoenix now is world renowned. Yet much of the world still has amusing misconceptions
about this city in the Valley of the Sun, and even the natives know
little of its astonishing background. Let's give it brief inspection.

One recent morning Adele and I decided that we needed water
on our small Phoenix rancho. We got it, at exactly the hour desired.
Rain? No, no — I simply went to the back fence and opened a ditch
valve. Four inches of water rushed onto our lawn, making a reflection pool of theatrical beauty. It mirrored the roses that adorn our
place every day in the year, the flowering vines that race up our walls,
the oranges beckoning like little suns in our patio, the oleander
blossoms banked like snow, and the tall wind-singing eucalyptus trees.
What we had done was routine, but it was also highly symbolic.

For in the valley where we live, man has built an incredible
oasis. Nowhere has he shown greater ingenuity in changing the face
of Nature and charting himself a better way of life. Rainfall here is
a scant six inches a year; yet on this scorched desert where "nothing"
grew, everything grows.

Here in our land, in our time, is the miracle of irrigation anew.

159

Its pattern is seen likewise in neighboring valleys — Casa Grande and Yuma in Arizona, Rio Grande in New Mexico and Texas, Imperial in California.

A two-pound trout splashed into our patio, with that controlled flood we so needed. We fried him for breakfast. One summer a friend of ours, sleeping in his back yard, was awakened at midnight by a flopping under his cot. He rolled over, and by the light of the moon throttled a twelve-pound catfish. The zanjero had turned his water in as ordered in advance.

Our children wade and sail their toy yachts on lakes in our yards. And yet these lakes subside in about three hours. Everywhere there is lush grass — which has eternally to be mowed. Dry air and the brilliant sun cooperate so that mud is no problem. We can have that four-inch lake, if we need it, every twelve days.

Our summer temperatures reach 120 degrees, and often three to six months pass without one drop of rain. Normally only cactus, mesquite, greasewood, catclaw and the like grow in this region. No cattle, not even the hardier sheep and goats, could be raised here before the ditch diggers came.

But around my home now are half a million acres where crops are harvested every month. In six weeks around Christmas time we ship ten thousand carloads of lettuce. Other vegetables, fruits, berries, hay, a long-staple cotton of premium value, even exotic dates, stream out of our valley by the trainloads. And cattle? We have today the biggest pen-feeding system in the world.

Why, then, are we not overrun by investors and opportunists?

We are! Just try to rent any sort of living quarters or any place to open an office, shop, or store in Phoenix. And as for the good earth — just try, indeed, to buy a farm within twenty miles of town. It will cost you a small fortune.

We have no indigent sharecroppers; the economics of our situation have simply ruled out poor tenant farmers. The officers of our banks are farmers. The chairman of the board of our biggest utility, and the president of our luxurious country club, both have

160

been farmers. The depression of 1929 was two years late here, and never virulent. Our business curve seems ever upward, our bank clearances seem always to climb. No less an economist than Roger W. Babson called this oasis "The Gold Spot of America."

Modern Phoenix is beyond anybody's "description" and the pattern of life here is so unusual, so surprising, that newcomers are enthralled. This holds, of course, for the whole Valley metropolitan area, including such jealously separate suburban units as Scottsdale, Tempe, Mesa, Glendale, Peoria, Litchfield. Newcomers, conditioned by hearsay or by Hollywood shallowness, come here expecting our symbol to be a lazy Mexican peon snoozing in the sun against a saguaro cactus. But, says the city's magazine, "The Valley shook the sand out of its toes decades ago and has been spurting to maturity with a speed that would shame Jack's beanstalk." This has included a multi-million-dollar building boom, with numerous new skyscrapers puncturing our azure sky, and with what are unmistakably the finest shopping centers in the world.

Thus it could be said accurately that the lazy-in-the-patio living pattern enjoyed by Adele and me is fruitful; nerved-up newcomers, highly successful somewhere else, come out here, slump on chaise longue or· hammock, wallow in pools, restore energy, then jump into sports clothes and get going again. Those who return to distant homelands are never satisfied there again, and the venturesome ones come back here to stay. They bring money and talent. They invest both, so that our cultural development keeps pace with the economic. So, our pattern of life is *not* one of languor; rather is it one of knowing when and how to relax, so as to restore energies for bigger doings. This very attitude has begotten one of this century's great metropoli.

Many individuals would have to be credited with the development of our oasis. But the conception of it — that visionary daydreaming by pioneers — came largely from a bride named Adaline. Let me now tell you her true story, as I got it directly from her and

161

other pioneers who knew her well, when *The Reader's Digest* assigned me to write a personality profile about her.

Early one morning in 1929 a plane landed by mistake near a farm home a mile southeast of the Phoenix business center. A little old woman saw it. Without waking relatives, she had slipped out this dawn to pet a new-born colt. She was barefoot, and she wore a tattered bathrobe. But when she saw the plane she had a sudden inspiration. She crawled quickly under a barbed wire fence and ran to the pilot.

"Could a body get a ride?" she greeted him eagerly. "It'd be a celebration. Today's my eighty-third birthday."

He beheld her face, checked deeply with the lines of much living; her hair, snowy and wind-blown and short as a child's. "Now I know where I am," said he. "This is the Gray mansion, for you are bound to be Adaline Gray."

Thus Adaline Gray, who on her honeymoon had ridden miles westward in a covered wagon, took her first and only flight over Arizona's Valley of the Sun. As a celebration it was entirely proper; she looked down on the rich desert oasis which she personally had done most to envision and pioneer. She saw the river, twisting through the midst of all that greenery like a fallen thread of sky. She saw five thousand miles of canals making silvery filigree. The gems sparkling on the green velvet were towns. One of them, the Phoenix which she herself had founded and controlled for four decades, had become a city of rare beauty. She came down from her flight beaming like a ten-year-old.

Arizona had been populated mainly by the Indians when Mrs. Gray first came west. But as the cactus was being cleared for Phoenix Village in 1870, she spoke up in meeting. "First public house you men build has got to be a school. We don't want our children to be brought up like little hellions. Get a teacher with some sense and pay him a fair wage."

She sat on horseback and made the bearded frontiersmen mind her. J. D. Daroche was brought in as schoolmaster at the unheard-of

162

salary of $100 a month; most teachers in that era got $15 to $40. Through the seventies and eighties Adaline Gray made frequent trips of inspection to see that the schools were progressing. She'd ride up to a window of the adobe schoolhouse, lean from her side-saddle, and shout in: "Everything all right? Need anything?" If firewood was low, if a desk was broken, if any child was backward, if spelling books were worn out, or if a teacher's ability seemed only mediocre, Adaline took action, on her own. Her precedent in demanding efficiency still holds. Today the Phoenix school system ranks among the best in the nation.

The roof of that first schoolhouse was completed on a Saturday noon, and Adaline promptly called a church meeting there for next day.

"Why shucks, Ma'am," a workman objected, "It ain't a soul in this valley that can preach."

"But every soul in this valley can pray," she countered.

When, later, the usual collection of bandits, gamblers, rustlers, and murderers drifted into booming Phoenix, Adaline Gray again went into action. One night when she was alone, a thief stole a saddle horse from in front of her house. She picked up a rifle. At about two hundred yards, by moonlight, she knocked him sprawling to the ground. She dragged him to her living room, doctored his wound, gave him dinner, and pointed down the road.

"Now git!" she ordered. "And if I ever catch you in Arizona again, I'll shoot and do no doctorin'."

That same week, two honest farmers were slain and robbed while on their way home from town. Nobody did much about it. Adaline thereupon saddled her horse and called on ten leading citizens. "Haven't you men got the stomach to clean up things?" she challenged. "You want us women to take over and run this valley?"

Shamed, they formed a vigilante group forthwith. They rounded up about fifty known or suspected outlaws, and the two who had murdered the farmers were identified. These they tied by the necks to a tree, then drove a wagon out from under them. With the bodies still dangling, and with an ominous crowd of citizens for spectators, the other undesirables were brought one by one to the wagon and noosed. As each pleaded for mercy he was given a canteen and told not to stop running until he crossed the Arizona line.

That became another precedent. Phoenix grew up renowned as a "Sunday-school town" — this in the same era and region that spawned Tombstone, Bisbee, Globe, Florence, and Prescott. Fine churches, with exceptional spiritual strength, dominate life in this Valley of the Sun today. Adaline Gray had brought her convictions westward with her.

Adaline was being reared in gentility on the Norris plantation, near Eldorado, Arkansas, before the War. One day Columbus Harrison Gray, handsome adventurer, came to say goodbye. "Gold boom on out West," he reminded them. "I'm headin' for Californy. Adaline — I declare if you aren't growing up fast!"

He went by sea, except for walking across the Isthmus of Panama. But he hurried back overland to fight for the Confederacy. When that travail was over, the Norris plantation had been destroyed and the South was heartbroken and without hope. Miss Adaline Norris was seventeen. "My, my!" Lum Gray whispered to her, this time in awe. "Nobody was ever so pretty and proud! Now out West, everything's clean and new and promisin'. I could scrape up mules . . . a wagon . . . if you —"

Lum Gray and Adaline Norris Gray dropped out of a wagon train after entering the Valley of the Sun in 1868. Weary of travel, Lum unhitched his mules near the Salt River to rest. He had heard about mineral wealth in Arizona and wanted to prospect, but Adaline, farm reared, beheld the valley with prophetic eye. "It's more gold in this soil than it is in the mountains," she told him. So while Lum, head in the clouds, took pick and shovel to hunt for ore, Adaline planted a little patch of turnip greens from seed in her wagon. By the time Lum returned, barren of nuggets, her greens were already edible. Lum hitched his two rested mules to a turning plow.

An adventurous bachelor named Jack Swilling had preceded the

164

Grays into the valley by a few months, and now lived in a brush lean-to. He had seen what the prehistoric Indians had accomplished by irrigation, and he yearned to emulate them. Jack was lazy and given to drink, and to morphine whenever he could get it. Even so, his judgment strengthened that of the Grays, who pitched in with him to clean out one old Indian canal. Jack sat on the bank and made pretty speeches, but did little physical labor. He would go hunting, and bring in game from the fine herds of deer, and coveys of the quail and doves that still abound in the region. And he'd play a *git*-tar and "sin-n-n-ng, law me, he could sing like the winds of morning," Aunt Adaline told us, decades later.

Travelers saw the Grays' water diversion, scoffed at first, then became interested. Many began to unhitch. Within twelve months a boom was on. Twelve more months and the village had a flour mill — Adaline Gray baked a cake from the first pound of wheat put through — the school, a church, two "right good" saloons, blacksmiths, an undertaker, a hotel at which "ladies without visible means of support may not register" (Jack Swilling said their names were always visible), two stores, and a butcher shop.

Adaline made the butcher hire an Indian boy to fan flies off his meat. Self-service was introduced. The butcher, Peter Holcomb, would hang half a steer carcass on his front porch and stick a knife in a post. Any customer could come by, cut off steaks or a roast to suit himself, then call through the door, "Charge me with about seven pounds, Pete."

Hundreds of acres had been brought under cultivation by the simple magic of turning water onto the thirsty earth. Adaline kept a measure out to catch the rain, and in the first two years scarcely nine inches fell. But away up the Salt, in the canyons beyond Four Peaks and Superstition Mountain, snow piled up a hundred feet deep before warm rains fell to melt it. Bountiful waters flowed down the river bed and were diverted onto farms by brush dams. The villagers grew fat, and the time came for a naming.

"As the phoenix, that bird of mythology, rose from its own

ashes," orated Darrell Duppa, in public meeting, "so will a great city rise here on the ashes of a past civilization. This valley once supported thousands of people. It will support thousands again. Let us name our town Phoenix."

"Talking through yore hat, ain't you, Lord Duppa?" Pump-handle John scoffed.

"Hush up," Adaline Gray ordered. "He's right. I bet a peck of potatoes I live to see ten thousand people here."

When she took her airplane ride Phoenix had a hundred and ten thousand population.

Once I sat with Aunt Adaline for hours while she showed me ancient arrowheads and pottery of the Hohokam. "A body has to respect the knowledge any people has in any time," she told me. "We advance, but we lose something when we do. Those ancient Indians were smarter in many ways than we are."

She was farming right where the Hohokam had farmed centuries before. With Lum making frequent trips to the hills, she had to defend the farm home alone. One night a band of Pimas came to steal her horses and mules. Her stable was a long adobe with flat roof and parapet walls. From ten at night until dawn she stayed up by the stable with her rifle.

"I'd shoot over the wall at one end, run and shoot over the other," she said, "and keep that up as long as they stayed close enough. I never knew how many I killed because they'd take their dead and wounded away when raiding. But I've always been a mighty good shot. When Lum got back, nary an animal was missing."

Lum Gray made a financial killing one year when he sold a mine for $60,000 cash, so Adaline made him build her a two-story red brick mansion near the river. It had ceilings fourteen feet high and seven bedrooms rich with oak panels and tinted glass transoms; and its great living room and halls soon were hallowed with memories. The landscaping included a swimming pool, a boating lake, rows of tall sentinel palms, rose gardens, flowering vines, bright green lawns for croquet courts and lovers' settees, and stables with high-stepping

166

horses and rubber-tired rigs. Adaline offered hospitality to friend and
stranger alike, so that the Gray mansion became the social and
political headquarters for this Territory of Arizona. Literally hundreds
of couples were married there, and brides often came back a year
later to have their babies there because of the loving care Adaline
could give them.

"There were times," the old lady recalled, "when forty or fifty
people would be guests in and around our house, and we all loved it.
Let me tell you a thing, son — there's nothing like friends! When our
beds filled, people would drop bedrolls on porches or in the yard.
Few came empty-handed. Buffalo meat, venison, wild turkey, all the
good things of the forest were ours. We'd doctor each other's sick,
bury our dead, bring lovers together and help them marry. Governors
and congressmen and little pigheaded politicians would come here and
make their plans sitting at our big table. Cowboys, miners, trappers,
travelers of every sort would stop just to visit.

"They liked to sit in our chairs hours on end, just looking at the
inside of my house. They'd get up and finger my window curtains, or
touch a lace doily like it would break. Why, they'd stand in front of
a vase of flowers or a pretty picture and just gawp at it, and handle a
book like it was holy. And if I played the piano for them — law,
their eyes would shine like panthers'! They were good men who led
rough lives, but heard about our place and came to see it. Once an old
wooly-bearded hunk of a mountain man tried to express his thanks
when he was leaving, and what do you think he said? 'Miz Gray,' he
said, 'it's been worth a fortune just to smell you.' I can understand
him, but I guess a lot of modern folks can't."

I can. He had found her sweet of person and sweet of mind,
just as I did half a century later. Aunt Adaline symbolized more than
she herself ever realized.

When she grew old she did not sit in a rocking chair and dream
of the past; I had to force reminiscences out of her. She'd sit when
she had to, but she wasn't feeling sorry for herself. I asked her what
she did think of.

167

"I'm studying about water," she explained. "We're already using all this Salt River water to tame our desert. But you listen here — that Colorado's a whopping big river. A body could ditch that water across Arizona to our valley lands. Our country's growing. People need more eatin' vegetables. If I just had my strength —"

Living in the past? She was pioneering in the future even though eighty years old, and here in the '60's her new dream is about to come true. She gave it impetus in her day, impetus that reached all the way to Washington. Twice she saw a great future for this city that Darrell Duppa said had risen out of the ashes of the past civilization here, yet even she could not have envisioned the oasis we know.

Nobody else could have envisioned it, either; the "possibilities" simply weren't here. For farming, yes, but farming alone doesn't make a vast metropolis. So what *did* make Phoenix burgeon in such spectacular manner, giving it momentum not likely to slow down in the next hundred years?

The only answer is — "a number of things." A city is as complex as an individual, and much like one in temperament. Farming was and will forever be a factor, yet farming itself has rapidly changed. Mining is a factor. So is manufacturing. So is that more nebulous something called culture — the fine arts of painting, music, theater, writing, sculpture, education, all the "sweeter subtleties" of life, including that most important of all, Christianity, for this truly is a town of fine churches and spiritual leadership. This is not to imply that Phoenix is perfect, indeed we have much to be ashamed of; but again that's normal, and as with any earnest individual we strive to correct it. Our good far outweighs our bad, and as to where the good comes from, there is only one possible over-all answer: the greater part of our city's magnificence comes directly or indirectly from that pervading influence, sunshine.

# XVI.  SUN SPOTS

## 1. The First Forty-Four

This volume has avoided slipping into that dull category known as "Tourist Guides." Nevertheless, experience proves that both the newcomer and the old-timer in Arizona do reach the moment when they appreciate suggestions for week-end outings and longer vacation tours, something a bit more specific than the open admonition to "get out and see the country." Hearing and reading about the southwestern storybook places quite naturally stimulates the desire to see them.

So here is an alphabetical list of delightful places to visit in Arizona — sunny spots in the sunniest, most "sight-seeable" state in the Union, with capsule descriptions and location helps. The list was prepared by and is copyrighted by the famed map makers, Rand McNally & Company, and is used here by their special permission.

1.  APACHE TRAIL — Beginning at Apache Junction, 34 miles east of Phoenix, this world-famous trail, once the dark and bloody stalking ground of the Apache, winds through gorgeous mountain scenery to Globe.

2. BARTLETT DAM — One of the highest of its type in the world, is on the Verde River, 193 feet above stream bed, 1,063 feet long at the crest. Storage capacity 182,608 acre feet. Approximately 55 miles from Phoenix via Cave Creek.

3. BOULDER (HOOVER) DAM — Seventy-two miles north of Kingman, the largest of all federal reclamation projects and one of the greatest feats of all time. The highest dam in the world, 727 feet high, reservoir 115 miles long, covering 227 square miles with a storage capacity of 30,500,000 acre feet.

4. CANYON DE CHELLY — NATIONAL MONUMENT — Near the New Mexico border, may be reached by good roads from Winslow, Holbrook, and Gallup, N. M. — Chinle Indian school is at the mouth of the canyon.

5. CARL PLEASANT DAM — A structure across the Agua Fria River, 35 miles northwest of Phoenix. The water impounded is used for irrigating the land to the south of the dam and east of the White Tank Mountains.

6. CASA GRANDE RUINS — NATIONAL MONUMENT — The well-preserved ruins of a four-storied prehistoric community dwelling near Coolidge, with remains of an extensive canal system. The "calendar" and maze found in the walls have excited the scholarly interest and speculation of archaeologists from all parts of the world.

7. CHIRICAHUA NATIONAL MONUMENT — Nature has fashioned a weird and silent community through the erosive agency of wind and water. Sometimes called Rhyolite Park or Wonderland of Rocks, this monument is located in Southeastern Arizona and may be reached from Douglas, Bisbee, Tombstone, or Willcox.

170

8. COCHISE STRONGHOLD — Seven miles from U. S. Highway 666, in the heart of the Dragoon Mountains. For many years the hiding place of the great Apache chief.

9. COLOSSAL CAVE — One of the state's wonders, 28 miles from Tucson and reached via U. S. 80, passing through Vail.

10. COOLIDGE DAM — Its waters are used to irrigate the Casa Grande Valley; it is situated on the Gila River 119 miles from Phoenix and 26 miles from Globe; height 250 feet; capacity 1,200,000 acre feet; largest multiple dome dam in the world.

11. DINOSAUR CANYON — Sixty miles north of Flagstaff, flanked by immense rocks on which are found tracks of the dinosaur.

12. FORTIFICATION MOUNTAIN — A spectacle of surpassing beauty, with flaming red base, black sides, and flat top. An excellent view may be had from Boulder Dam — Kingman Highway.

13. GRAND CANYON — NATIONAL MONUMENT AND PARK — The world's greatest natural wonder. For two hundred miles the Colorado River flows through this great canyon, appearing a mere thread when viewed from the rim a mile above. No words have been found adequate to describe the breath-taking beauty of this spectacle.

14. GRAND FALLS — Southeast of Cameron on the Little Colorado River. Falls and rapids of great scenic beauty.

15. HOPI INDIAN VILLAGES — Walpi, Oraibi, Hotevilla, Chimopovi, etc., where the annual and world-famous snake dance is held late in July and early August. These villages may be reached from Holbrook or Winslow.

16. HORSE MESA DAM — Forming Apache Lake, 60 miles from Phoenix, the first of the chain of lakes below Roosevelt Dam.

17. METEOR CRATER — Regarded as one of Arizona's strangest wonders, formed by the landing of some visitor from outer space. It is 21 miles west of Winslow.

171

18. MISSION SAN XAVIER DEL BAC — Located nine miles south of Tucson, this mission is conceded to be the most beautiful mission structure in the Southwest. Established 1700.

19. MONTEZUMA CASTLE — NATIONAL MONUMENT — Its history shrouded in the mist of centuries, is located 54 miles east of Prescott, in the Verde Valley. A cliff dwelling.

20. MONTEZUMA WELL — A cup-shaped lake, 78 feet below the surrounding terrain, 750 feet in diameter, and fed by subterranean waters.

21. MORMON FLAT DAM — Forming Canyon Lake, 47 miles from Phoenix and second in the Salt River Irrigation Project chain of reservoirs below Roosevelt.

22. NATURAL BRIDGE — Fourteen miles north of Payson and three miles from the main highway. A scenic wonder which yearly attracts many tourists.

23. NAVAHO BRIDGE — Seven miles below the historic Lee's Ferry. The bridge floor is 467 feet above the water level of the Colorado River, the span across being 616 feet in length.

24. NAVAHO NATIONAL MONUMENT — Eighty miles from Flagstaff, one of the interesting features of the Navaho Indian reservation. Many prehistoric Indian ruins, ancient caves, and cliff dwellings delight the scientist and historian.

25. OAK CREEK CANYON — Located in the eastern part of Yavapai County and the southern part of Coconino County, a favorite resort of the angler. Is accounted to be second only in beauty and marvelous coloring to the Grand Canyon.

26. ORGAN PIPE CACTUS — NATIONAL MONUMENT — South of Ajo and bordering on Mexico. This cactus is so named because its branches resemble the pipes of the pipe organ. It grows

as much as 20 feet tall and is one of the uncommon species of the cactus family.

27. PAINTED DESERT — Here Nature has swung a reckless brush and painted the sands of the mountainsides in gorgeous hues. This famous scenic attraction may be viewed from Highway 66.

28. PETRIFIED FOREST — NATIONAL MONUMENT — About 20 miles east of Holbrook, where the petrified remains of prehistoric trees, some as large as 250 feet in length, blend in gorgeous hues.

29. PIPE SPRING — NATIONAL MONUMENT — One of Arizona's historical and picturesque spots. In the early pioneering days this section was the scene of many struggles between settlers and outlaws.

30. PUEBLO GRANDE — Ancient Indian ruin near Phoenix, extensively excavated, flourished about 1200 A.D.

31. RAINBOW BRIDGE — NATIONAL MONUMENT — Located 190 miles north of Flagstaff (in Utah). The bridge is 309 feet high and has a span of 278 feet across Bridge Canyon.

32. ROOSEVELT DAM — One of the first federal reclamation projects, located 79 miles from Phoenix via the Apache Trail. The dam is 273 feet high and forms a lake 25 miles in length.

33. SACRAMENTO PIT — Located at Bisbee, is one of the largest mines of its kind in the world. More than 20,000,000 tons of copper ore have been taken from this mine.

34. SAGUARO NATIONAL MONUMENT — Near Tucson, where the government has set aside 63,284 acres in order to preserve the Giant Cactus which is typical of Arizona, the bloom of which is the state flower.

35. SAN FRANCISCO MOUNTAINS — Near Flagstaff, they tower over the surrounding plateau country at an elevation of 12,600 feet above sea level.

173

36. SOUTHWESTERN ARBORETUM — Between Florence Junction and Superior. Unique wonderland of plant life. Ten thousand varieties of plants from every continent are here assembled.

37. STEWART MOUNTAIN DAM — Forming Saguaro Lake. The dam is 1,260 feet long and 212 feet in height.

38. SUNSET CRATER — NATIONAL MONUMENT — A cone-shaped crater of volcanic cinder, near Flagstaff, gray at the base and tapering to a red tip, which reflects the rays of the sun with gorgeous effect.

39. TOMBSTONE — One of the most famous mining towns in the West, at the height of its glory it was a city of equal importance with San Francisco.

40. TONTO NATIONAL MONUMENT — Prehistoric cliff dwellings in an excellent state of preservation, located just east of Roosevelt Dam on the Apache Trail.

41. TUMACACORI MISSION — NATIONAL MONUMENT — Established in 1690 by the Jesuit priest, Father Kino, the ruins of this structure show the Spanish influence characteristic of all missions built throughout the Southwest.

42. TUZIGOOT NATIONAL MONUMENT — A pre-Columbian ruin dating about 1300 A.D., two miles east of Clarkdale on the east bank of the Verde River.

43. WALNUT CANYON — NATIONAL MONUMENT — Many cliff dwellings make this one of the most interesting points in the state, within easy driving distance of Flagstaff.

44. WUPATKI — NATIONAL MONUMENT — Between Flagstaff and Tuba City, the government has set aside 35,865 acres for the preservation of the prehistoric Indian ruins found in this Monument.

\* \* \*

One more "spot" must be added, because of its sheer novelty if nothing else. That's HAVASU CANYON. It holds "the lowest-down people on earth," 200 or so Havasupai Indians in a village at the bottom of the Grand Canyon. It is exceedingly picturesque and colorful, even to the high blue waterfall there, which inspired a famous song. The village is an eight-mile walk or muleback ride from where you park your car. Nowadays building materials and heavy furniture are delivered by helicopter. But life there is pure Shangri La, isolated, astonishing, wonderful. Go and see.

## 2. Ten Memorable Days of Seeing

Any one of those forty-five sun spots, and sometimes several of them (depending on your location) may be seen in a few hours or a week-end trip. But many folk want a longer run, something that can be packaged neatly into a two-week vacation, that can hold high value in both education and recreation without outrageous cost.

So then, I present my favorite sun-country tour, ten exciting days. For sheer astonishment, for scenery of breathless beauty, for storybook lore and all-around gee-whiz quality at minimum cost, this cannot be excelled on our continent. The roads are superb, the accommodations topflight. Train, plane, and bus services are excellent. Roads are open the year round. You'll need no fancy clothes; sports outfits or "westerns" are right, plus comfortable walking shoes. Bring warm sweaters or jackets for chilly summer nights in high altitudes, and in winter bring your heaviest things. Rain equipment won't be out of place. Include a vacuum jug for water in arid stretches, and a can for emergency gasoline in the far-back areas. Field glasses, cameras (color film by all means), and notebooks will add to the pleasure.

Note that the routing is not limited to political boundaries but stretches into a friendly neighboring state; indeed Arizona Territory once was a part of New Mexico Territory, so similar are they in terrain and other interests. These two states truly are *the Southwest*. Mores and manners are much the same in each; crossing the state line thus brings you a bonus.

Write two places in advance: The Arizona State Highway Department, Phoenix, and the New Mexico State Tourist Bureau, Santa Fe. Ask each to mail you its free souvenir map of the state. These are expensively done, beautiful enough for framing, educational, accurate, alluring. Note that you can start your tour from any direction with almost equal ease, but your planning must take into consideration your home base. People in western or northern Arizona, and friends from California, naturally would start the tour at Hoover Dam. But the records show that most sight-seeing travelers come from the east, so for our hypothetical ten days we begin here at that underground wonder-of-wonders, Carlsbad Caverns in New Mexico.

Make Carlsbad reservations in advance in summer; it's a good-sized town but tourists do crowd in. There are fine swimming pools for refreshing yourself there, and motel costs are reasonable.

Now for our exact logging:

*First day.* Mileage today: only 167, all in the afternoon. But arise early and be at the entrance to Carlsbad Caverns by 8 A.M. This is twenty miles from the town, so allow time. For a small fee, the National Park Service gives you expert guide service, leads you down hundreds of stairsteps into a veritable mystery kingdom. All other known caves shrink in importance when compared to Carlsbad.

Don't fear the walking. It is taken in easy stages with frequent rests. Walk down, take the elevator up, for the full show. If you do miss the 8-o'clock trip down, others follow at intervals throughout the morning. The earlier trips will get you out in ample time for a leisurely run down U. S. 62 and 180 to El Paso, with time to see it that afternoon.

This is a "different" city, so enjoy it. Ride up the Mount Franklin trail and have your look at Mexico, across the Rio Grande. Sister city over there is Juarez. Drive down to the international

176

bridge, park your car, and walk or ride the bus over. This saves red tape. You need no passport, no changing to Mexican money.

Visit the ancient Juarez cathedral, the market place, the jail, the alluring shops. It is "correct" to haggle genially with the merchants; compare prices, then make your offer, for souvenirs. None of the eating and drinking places in Juarez is recommended for the average American tourist family. Much of the glamour here is synthetic; the real Mexico starts farther south of the border.

Sleep in El Paso or nearby. This city has many fine hotels and courts. Reservations are seldom necessary, but they are comforting to have, especially on weekends.

*Second day.* Mileage: about 420, on main route. Head north on U. S. 80 and 85 for Las Cruces. Three miles short of Cruces at Mesilla is a museum "honoring" Billy the Kid, a pioneer-day murderer. The Spanish or Mexican influence is strong now. It's a place to begin refreshing your interest in history of the Wild West. Time and money permitting, you can advantageously linger for visits to many historic sites during this entire trip. Leave Las Cruces on U. S. 70 and 80 and continue via Deming.

At Lordsburg an important choice confronts you. Our main route is logged first, the alternate route will follow.

Main route westward: stick on U. S. 70. In the early afternoon you will roll over Coolidge Dam, which stores water for irrigation. This is Apache Indian country. At Globe and Miami you'll see picturesque mining towns; Arizona is the foremost copper-producing state. Those smoke-belching "factories" are ore smelters. Those strange artificial hills, black or yellowish, are wastes from ore reduction.

Follow U. S. 70 via Superior. This is one of the world's most scenic stretches of highway; deep canyons, bridges from peak to peak, tunnels, lavish color everywhere. Three miles west of Superior is the Southwestern Arboretum, a collection of the many strange plants

177

that adorn the desert. Admission is free, and walk-through time averages one hour.

At Florence Junction keep to the right. On your right horizon now is world-renowned Superstition Mountain, which conceals the Lost Dutchman Gold Mine. You haven't time to stop and search, but pause at Apache Junction to photograph the monument to the Dutchman with Superstition for a background.

By now you will have observed the remarkable desert flora. That big candlestick thing, 10 to 40 feet tall, is the saguaro (sah-WAH-ro), the world's largest cactus. It grows only in Arizona and in Sonora, Mexico, though eastern artists persistently locate it in every state from Texas to Oregon, thus making it a main symbol of the West. Its beautiful white blossom, seen in June, is the Arizona state flower. In July this becomes an edible red fruit, much favored by the Indians. More than 600 other species of cactus grow in the area, most with extraordinarily colorful and gorgeous blossoms, seen from March through August. Similarly interesting growths, often mistaken for cacti, are the ocotillo, the *maguey* or century plant, the yucca, plus the famed mesquite, palo verde, and ironwood trees.

You are now in Arizona's famed Valley of the Sun. Near Mesa you see the irrigation canals — from reservoirs on the Salt River (which is not salty), formed by a series of huge dams. They turn the desert into a garden of about 350,000 extremely valuable farm acres. Better not belittle any summer "warmth" — which may touch 112 degrees. This insures a crop every month of the year, and makes this valley a winter resort. (Other water sources add to the total irrigated acreage here).

That odd square building on your left at Mesa is a Mormon temple, well worth a visit. Then push on through Tempe (Arizona State University), over the Salt River past the beautiful Desert Botanical Garden, lush green golf courses (one lighted for night play), resort style motels, and on into the state capital, Phoenix.

In summer you need no reservations to get fine air-conditioned hotel or motel space; in winter you do. Tonight, drive to the end of

South Central Avenue and up the skyline trail to the world's largest municipal park. From Lookout Point gaze down on the lighted metropolis, greatest oasis in the world. Or drive north and take Lincoln Drive for a comparable night view.

*Alternate route from Lordsburg to Phoenix.* Added mileage: about 150.

Take this alternate route if you can allocate one additional day.

At Lordsburg, the alternate route turns *left.* After 17 miles, this one branches. This second left turn, on U. S. 80, leads to the Mexican border town of Douglas and Bisbee, thence on to the wildest town the Wild West ever knew — Tombstone. Here you must see the old O. K. Corral where the Earps and the Clantons fought their duel, the Bird Cage Theatre, the Boot Hill Cemetery, loaded with outlaws and saints.

Up the road about 75 miles is Tucson (too-SAHN). Spend the night; no reservations necessary in summer. Visit the University of Arizona here, a beautiful campus. Nearby is historic San Xavier, one of the grandest in the chain of missions established by Spanish missionaries. Here, too, is an authentic reproduction of *old* Tucson, a movie set, now a museum.

After lunch in Tucson, drive up State 84 to Picacho, take a right turn onto State 87, and stop at America's first skyscraper — Casa Grande (CAH-sah GRAHN-day: meaning "big house"). It's a national monument, a four-story structure with village walls around it, possibly the finest of our prehistoric ruins. After the tour and lecture, push on via 87 into Mesa, thence into Phoenix. (End of alternate route from Lordsburg.)

*Third day.* Mileage: about 285. Take a quick drive around Phoenix in the cool early morning. Include the Camelback Mountain area where you'll see famous resort hotels, date orchards, orange, grapefruit, lemon, and olive groves, alfalfa and cotton fields, many fine estates. Note the newness of the city, the Spanish- and Ranch-

179

style homes, the irrigated fields and lawns. Then on U. S. 89, head northwest for Prescott.

Past the town of Wickenburg, dude-ranch capital of the world, you'll climb suddenly up Yarnell Hill into a new, cool climate. Prescott is a mile high, a center for cowboys, miners, trappers, vacation resorts. Push on, via *Alternate* 89 — careful to take the correct turn for this — through Granite Dells (many two-gun movies are filmed here) to the astonishing ghost town of Jerome. This once-thriving mining community is largely abandoned, and is slipping downhill or caving into underground mine shafts.

(You could of course go on the newer Black Canyon Highway No. 69 to Prescott; it's wider, faster. But remember, you aren't "going somewhere" on this trip, you are sight-seeing! Old 89 is in excellent condition and will reward you for its extra hour or so.)

About six miles beyond Jerome, near Clarkdale, pause for a look at Tuzigoot (TOOT-se-goot), an Indian word meaning Crooked Waters, from the stream nearby. This national monument is one of the most impressive prehistoric villages, much of it intact or restored, well worth an hour. Two miles farther on, near the village of Clemenceau, watch for a big sign turning you to the right to see Montezuma Castle National Monument. This is a scenic 30-minute side trip, showing you an incredible way of life as of about 800 years ago. Rangers on duty will answer your questions.

Back on Alternate 89, proceed to Sedona and up Oak Creek Canyon. Here you'll go color-film crazy, for the reds, yellows, greens, and blues of the landscape are "impossible" though real. Push on to Flagstaff, turn left on U. S. 66-89 toward Williams, take a sudden right turn at the entry gate that points you to the Grand Canyon.

Reservations at Grand Canyon are a must, any time of year. Bright Angel Lodge and cabins are recommended; they have a wide price range, from campsites on up to luxury. Don't be surprised if pet deer, squirrels, chipmunks, and birds come right into your cabin, begging food. Park rangers advise that you leave dogs, cats, and guns at home.

*Fourth day.* No "description" of the Grand Canyon will be attempted, because its impact defies any adequate phrasing. After lunch, drive the few miles westward on the Rim Trail to Hermit's Rest, going onto every point for a thrilling view. Get back to El Tovar in time for the daily Indian dances, usually about 5 P.M. (check the time for them before you leave). Then go back to the rim for the sunset. Sleep here again, but enjoy the movies and lectures before bedtime.

*Fifth day.* Mileage: about 300. After breakfast, drive eastward on the Rim Trail, again making all the prescribed stops, but especially at Grand View and Hopi Tower. Then follow this highly picturesque road on to Cameron, where you turn southward on U. S. 89. Four miles short of Flagstaff, turn east again on U. S. 66. Winslow, 158 miles from Grand Canyon, is a good lunch stop. Then clip along another 57 miles to the signs that mark the Painted Desert and Petrified Forest.

A small entry fee is charged at Petrified Forest. You are only 73 miles from your next sleep, Gallup. Summer reservations in Gallup are essential; make them through its Chamber of Commerce, well in advance.

*Sixth day.* Mileage: about 200. Gallup is "Indian head-quarters." With emergency food, water, and gasoline in your car, let's see some really *wild* west. North from Gallup just eight miles, turn west on State 68 to Ganado, Arizona (gah-NAH-doe).

Ganado is a Presbyterian Mission village developed by the internationally renowned "sagebrush surgeon," Dr. Clarence Salsbury. It has the finest Indian schools and hospital. You will be on the Navaho reservation. Those moundlike homes of mud and logs are called hogans (HO-gahns). You may visit the families in them if you move slowly, smile, and act as courteous as they are. Drive on up to Chinle (chin-LEE) and see the incomparable Canyon de Chelly (SHAY-e) with its White House Cliff Dwellings, its weird monuments and colors. Then you must return via Ganado. You are about as far from "civilization" in this area as it is possible to get in the United States. Do not attempt any side trips or exploring without a guide and full provisions. Sleep again in Gallup.

*Seventh day.* Mileage: about 160. Head east on U. S. 66. You're still in the colorful country of the Indians, especially of the pueblo dwellers (PWEB-lo, *not* pew-ebb-lo). About 80 miles east of Gallup, just after you pass Grants, take the right turn that leads to the strangest townsite in America — Acoma (AH-ko-mah).

This is a sky city. It is on a rock table 400 feet up, known since Coronado discovered it in 1504, still inhabited. Don't rush; this is a timeless town. A small fee is charged, but your welcome depends on your courtesy rather than your money or "importance."

Acoma is only 60 miles from your next sleep — Albuquerque (that rhymes with turkey, not kirk). Have reservations, by all means; Chamber of Commerce will send you a list of recommended places.

*Eighth day.* Put these "musts" on your list for a one-day stay in Albuquerque: the University of New Mexico, extraordinary for its beautiful, Spanish-pueblo architecture; the zoo of Western wildlife; "Old Town" Plaza where Albuquerque was begun in 1705, with many of its historic buildings, art museums, quaint shops, and eating places. Most of the houses are adobe (ah-DOE-bay: native mud, sunbaked into large bricks). The Chamber will give you routings of many interesting one-day loop trips into highly scenic country. Sleep again in Albuquerque.

*Ninth day.* Mileage: about 75. Take U. S. 85 northward to Bernalillo (ber-nah-LEE-yo). Just across the fabled Rio Grande here is Coronado Monument, ruins of Kuaua where Coronado camped in 1540. Within 30 miles are several other highly picturesque Indian pueblo villages. From Bernalillo you are only 45 paved miles to the old and justly famous *La Villa Real de la Santa Fe de San*

182

*Francisco de Asis.* Yankee "efficiency" has boiled that lovely name down to a nub — Santa Fe.

This is not merely a city. It is a way of life. Its influence extends through all the Southwest. Its tempo is leisurely, graceful, courteous — and strange. The adobe construction, the pueblo styling already encountered, comes to a climax here; Santa Fe is *all* Spanish-pueblo. It was founded in 1610 by the governor of New Spain, and his palace is still a wondrous place to visit. Sleep in Santa Fe. Advance reservations are essential.

*Tenth day.* Mileage: about 80. Extend your Santa Fe visit through this morning, but toward noon drive up toward U. S. 64 to that town of almost equal fame — Taos (towss). Here is the grandest of all Indian pueblos — with a welcome mat out for pale-faces. Here is America at the peak of its aboriginal culture, little changed since 1492. Give the local chieftain his fee, then take your color pictures, ask questions.

The white village of Taos also is fascinating. This, included in what Santa Fe claims is the most interesting 50-mile square in America, is a main reason for calling New Mexico the Land of Enchantment.

From Taos, work homeward as you will. Three main roads lead out — two northward, into the matchless Rocky Mountain scenery of Colorado, one branching eastward at Raton thence on into Oklahoma and Texas. The third leads back to Santa Fe, with routes in all directions from there.

Scant mention has been made of the rich historical lore on every side of every highway; inquire for it wherever you pause, and prepare yourselves through advance reading.

Also, literally hundreds of special events are scheduled each year — fiestas, rodeos, art exhibits, lectures, guided trips, Indian dances, carnivals, fairs. Get lists from each local chamber of commerce, and enjoy them as your scheduling permits. But if you

183

do no more than follow the routing here, you will have one of the most memorable vacations of your life.

Note, again, that this is a circle tour; you can take all or any part of it and be richly rewarded, starting from any point. Some folk like to do the northern high-altitude parts in summer and the lower, warmer parts in winter. Whatever you choose, drive with relaxed, happy mental attitude, thus avoiding tourist fatigue.

\*   \*   \*

Now we must pay tribute to a section of Arizona that all too often is neglected in travel brochures, illustrated lectures and such, a region that is something of an empire unto itself because of its location. This is the Yuma area.

Yuma is so full of legend and lore and history that even the Yumans can't keep informed. The city and area suffers some because the low altitude and humidity there does indeed make summers a bit uncomfortable. Even so, as throughout southern Arizona, refrigerated buildings and cars have made tremendous impact. The soil is rich, the water is there, and so prosperity abides. The scenery is not the best. And yet, what is scenery? Isn't it, in fact, relative? If you measure it by what two-thirds of the nation has to offer, Yuma's scenery is superb. Her sunsets alone can send poets and artists into ecstasies.

Most famous "attraction" tourists know about there is of course the old Territorial Gaol, the prison that held many notorious criminals in the wild west days. It was "escape proof" although prisoners escaped. Go there now, see the ancient cells cut from solid rock, enjoy the fine museum values on display, hear the incredible true stories.

Share, too, the unique recreation facilities of this area. This centers around the Colorado River, which swirls under the great bridge linking us with California there; boating and fishing and skiing and swimming deluxe. This also is the only part of the state where you can study sea birds regularly, egrets especially. Imperial

184

Dam, 19 miles upriver from Yuma, is a mecca for bird lovers from all over the nation. Probably it has the largest population of tree swallows, in season, of any place on the continent. These birds emerge in early morning and spend a happy day on the wing, catching insects.

The Yuma area, then, is one more asset for us all to enjoy.

## Ride to the Rainbow

Repeatedly on other pages I have told you that Arizona is rainbow country; that its colors are fantastic, beyond imagining in their brilliance and their impact on human emotions. Mention was made of Oak Creek Canyon, Grand Canyon, Vermillion Cliffs, Superstition, and truly they are spectacular. But these exhibits are *known,* so much that we too often take them for granted, failing to appreciate their magnificence because we stream past them by the millions.

Is there, then, some isolated area, some hidden color treasure which the modern adventurer can visit only by going out of the routine tourist routing? Some magical rainbow land where picture postcard and souvenir stands don't clutter the foreground?

There is!

It is precisely that — a region of magic, shimmering with rainbow tints and hues, hidden from all crass materialists as a fairy-land should be. Early in 1964 I wrote of it for *Empire Magazine,* a Denver *Post* supplement (which has kindly granted permission to reprint here), and hundreds of thousands of folk were intrigued but skeptical. Yet I repeat, there *is* a fairyland of color in Arizona little known to white men but accessible to the daring. Ride with me, then, along the rainbow trail . . . . .

In a certain big book in a metal box on a rock table in the wildest, least civilized region of the United States you'll find my family registered — Nos. 6391-2-3-4. Back further in the book

185

you'll find the signatures and numbers of such adventurers as Zane Grey, John D. Rockefeller, Jr., Irvin S. Cobb, Theodore Roosevelt. Considerable effort was necessary to get to this spot. The last fifteen miles required eight hours on mule or horseback. But the strain was infinitely worth while, for that book rests under the world's most incredibly beautiful rainbow, petrified in shimmering stone.

My family has done more than 160,000 miles of American sightseeing, and we agree that nothing even approaches the grandeur of that rainbow ride. Those famous folk said the same thing.

This greatest of arches, we learned, was not meant to be seen by the roller-coaster-thrill-seeking hordes of tourists. We left the highway near Cameron, Arizona, rolled easily to Tuba City. But the next ninety miles took us six hours during which we saw only two human beings, one a bearded prospector and the other a Navaho on a horse. We were in a wilderness so primitive that we forgot civilization entirely.

The twisting road that slowed down our car happily slowed down our minds and nerves as well; we couldn't whiz by things, we had time to look and meditate and enjoy. Moreover, that area has abundant interest — some of the most inspired scenery in this world. The long, *long* vistas, the upthrusts and canyons and cliffs, the isolation, the unbelievable wealth of colors everywhere, the high-altitude air zinging through your lungs — these qualities make terrific impact. They hold for all of this trip. Many closeups are like some zany artist's conceptions for a stage set.

Typically, on the map is a dot labeled "Elephant's Feet." Here they are indeed, perfect to the last toe, but they are skyscraper size and of solid stone. Temptation is to use all your color photo film on this approach. Restrain yourself, for this is but the opening of what is to be a magnificent symphony lasting at least three days.

Our first goal was Navaho Mountain, near the Utah line. When we got there we had the feeling of adventure already done; if we never went anywhere else, this alone would be memorable. We ate and rested here. We met Lisbeth Eubank, the astonishing "white

186

goddess" who has dedicated her life to serving the few wild and proud Indians of this region. Our host for the evening was a westerner with many talents and personality facets. We slept in his beds that night, only vaguely aware that our adventure hadn't really begun.

After breakfast we were immediately shunted into saddles. There were nine in our party and some were not horse minded, indeed were the softest of city dudes. That didn't matter. We were instructed just to sit quietly and let the animals do the thinking.

Being farm reared, I chose a mule; a mule has twice as much sense as any horse, and more stamina. My Adele rode a mule next behind me, as a good squaw should. Our sixteen-year-old Rosemary was on a golden steed, and eleven-year-old Gail on a high-stepping paint. They promptly maneuvered themselves up front next to the guide in order to belabor him with questions. Happily, he was used to banter, he could take and he could dish it out. Being youngish and handsome in his cowboy togs did not hurt his prestige.

"Hyah-hyah!" he yelled to the animals, and they moved out like a rough herd. He had a lead rope on Old Meg. She seemed like a 900-year-old mule. She was loaded to the gunnels with food and stuff and she almost had to be dragged, her neck stretched as if about to be pulled out by the roots. This kept up for hours, then suddenly the guide unsnapped Meg's rope and set her free.

"How come?" I demanded. "If she was so reluctant, won't she run back home with our grub now?"

"Nawp," said the man. "She knows we've passed the halfway point, knows it's closer this way now to her feed. She'll lead us the rest of the way."

She did, too; I told you mules were smart.

Navaho Mountain itself is 10,416 feet high, and all around it for at least a hundred miles is pure, spectacular beauty. Erosion has been at work here since God said, "Let the earth take form," and Nature has done rare experimenting with her chisels and her paints. She goofed on a lot of colossal ceramics, and just tossed them aside. There's a surprise for every hundred yards.

187

We exclaimed, "Look! Look there!" to one another for the first half mile or so, but gradually it all overwhelmed us and we subsided. Voices became hushed. Work, taxes, wars, home worries, all were forgotten. Grown men and women were choked with a new and exhilarating kind of emotion.

The fifteen-mile trail is rugged. But it is enthralling if you concentrate on the vast and beautiful panorama slowly unfolding as the animals move. The first hour we crossed four canyons, each deeper than the last. We paused atop a mesa touching the sky, glanced back for a last hint of the world we remembered — a dot of smoke, somewhere. We turned right, and the guide silently pointed; yonder were two huge mountain lions on a ledge. They studied us with haughty disdain before ambling away.

Suddenly my mule angled down. I looked between his ears and saw our trail 2,000 feet below us. He had to take a hairpin turn on a rocky ledge not three feet wide, but apparently he became intrigued with this lookout view. He planted front hoofs at the edge and hung over it.

Now, a mule is a rare critter at best, built much like a bomber plane with a bulk of its fuselage well in front of its landing gear. I could spit into eternity, right past my saddle horn. If I'd fallen here it would not have killed me — I'd have starved to death before I hit bottom. I decided the mule was contemplating a suicide plunge.

But no; slowly, tantalizingly, surefootedly, after six seconds that seemed six hours, he went on down trail. I resumed breathing. This experience was to be repeated many times during the next forty-eight hours; it's just an old mule custom. Right now the trail widened, the guide looked around grinning and shouted, "Everybody all right?"

His question was flung back at us from at least a dozen cliffs — "RIGHT? . . . Right? . . . Right? . . . right?"

My kids were popeyed. So was their mother. She smiled at me, spurred up to ride stirrup-to-stirrup and hold my hand a moment. There were no words. None was necessary. Whenever there is any particularly moving experience thus shared and enjoyed, a touch is all we need.

The bottom of this great canyon is graced by millions of trees, shrubs, grasses, evergreens. There's a strange "lead bush" loaded with what appear to be silver dimes. There's quinine bush and Mormon tea or ephedrine, and giant cedars no end, all along the trail. We crossed and re-crossed a stream which seemed so blue it could dye a handkerchief. All around now were walls hundreds of feet high, bright pink, red, salmon, yellow, or mixtures of these. Often there were colored layers making giant cakes, the icing a fall-over of chocolate or cocoanut beginning far above.

We dismounted here, lay on our bellies to drink of the icy water, ate hearty lunches, then flopped supine in the sand. I was dead for thirty minutes. I'd be sleeping yet except that the guide goaded us up. We were astonishingly refreshed. And, again, what we'd seen was mere prologue to what was to come. The afternoon's scenery was grander than the morning's, building that visual symphony to climax after climax.

Often we rode single file through crevasses in pink-red rock mountains that held an eerie luminescence in the sun. Our path would be so narrow we could stretch our arms and touch the walls on either side; so deep that the sky was a thread of blue light. We were Lilliputians in a Brobdingnagian land. We'd move into circus arenas colossal in size, and there sure enough would be the animals. We saw the stone elephant that had lost those feet — an absolutely perfect head, ears, trunk, tusks, the size of a 40-story building.

There's a lion whose mane was molten yellow rock flowing down an antediluvian hill; and bears no end; and a wolf with teeth exposed; and several Indian chieftains' heads, all carved in ancient stone. Once I went into the bushes and behind a log found a spotted fawn, very much alive but motionless. I tiptoed out, knowing Mother Doe was near and anxious. Later through a rock window we saw four bucks bounding off. But all day we saw no other human beings, no hint of mankind's doings except our crude trail.

189

By midafternoon we felt fatigued; not physically, for the guide gave us frequent rests and walked us some to avoid stiffness, but emotionally. I dozed in the saddle for the last half hour. Glassy-eyed, I felt the train circling a great red cliff, and suddenly up front somewhere my youngest chick let out a yell. All of us turned the bend and reined up.

There it was.

The Rainbow, trapped here by the rock mountains, itself petrified, arched magnificently, brilliantly pink in the waning sun.

An "artificial" carving it was, for it seemed unnatural though Nature made it, laboring on it these many millions of years. A natural bridge, yet unlike any other anywhere. Most natural bridges are flat on top, really just holes in a cliff. This one stands apart, a rainbow in shape, curved and 40 feet thick in its crest.

Its proportions are so nearly perfect that it dwarfs all human architecture of the sort. It is 309 feet high, hence could span the dome of the capitol in Washington and have room to spare. It is one and a half times higher than the Bunker Hill Monument in Boston. Its span is 278 feet across a clear, icy creek.

We rode up to it, under it, quiet as mice. The fatigue was gone now. But the excitement was restrained. Impact of the Rainbow is like that of a great cathedral, though much more grand.

Twilight had begun when we filed back around the bend for the night's rest. The guide shooed us away; he did all the cooking. Camp was in a gigantic Navaho hogan also carved by nature, a circular red-rock auditorium hundreds of feet across, perfect in acoustics, with a high overhanging roof all around, with water and wood at hand.

Bedding and some food had been cached there earlier. The animals were freed but, sensing our fellowship, ate their grain then grazed close by. My family and I snuck off, walked half a mile, stripped naked and bathed in that creek under the Rainbow. Pools were no more than belly deep and were loaded with millions of tiny fish — appropriately, rainbow trout. These were so hungry they attached themselves to our legs, by the dozens, to our girls' shivery

190

delight. We went back to camp, ate incredible quantities of food, and hit the bedrolls by 9 P.M.

At midnight I was roundly nuzzled and kissed on the face. My mule had come up to love me — a common thing on this trail. He had adopted me, and spent most of the night at my side. My Babe's paint horse stood guard over her, too, and it was all somehow satisfying. The guide snored like two panthers fighting. Somehow everything seemed just right.

We rode back leisurely next day, though many persons stay longer. We'd had all we could absorb. Lunch on the trail again was delightful, but the heavy dinner back at the dining room was more so. Exhausted? Mom and I were ready to rest after that thirty miles of up-and-down-and-twist, but I remembered our kids — "May we ride on down to the corral with the guide, just for fun?" they begged. "It's only a half mile." Kids are nuts; they can take anything. Some as young as four have made this Rainbow ride with no trouble at all. One woman in our party was aged seventy-eight.

The Rainbow was merely a legend for centuries, a tall tale told by a few Indians. In 1909, a Piute led Dr. Byron Cummings, distinguished archaeologist, through the long maze of cliffs and canyons right to the place. News of this smoked out friends of W. L. Douglass, a federal surveyor, claiming *he* was the first white man to see the bridge. So who-was-first is controversial, among whites. But in 1927 Mr. and Mrs. John Wetherill, pioneers in northern Arizona, quietly settled the issue and shamed both claimants by erecting a bronze plaque at the bridge honoring Nashja-begay, the Indian "who first guided the white man" to the Rainbow.

"Barahoini" the Piute Indian called the Rainbow, and this has become a password for our clan, the fortunate few who have since been there. The good professor came out rhapsodizing about this world wonder.

So will you. It is guaranteed to color your memories and your conversation for the remainder of your life.

(To see Rainbow Bridge, write or telephone Rainbow Lodge,

191

or Navaho Mountain School, via Tuba City, Arizona, for reservations and guides.)

## New Mystery Kingdom

Finally, in our Arizona sight-seeing, the time has come to go underground.

This is "new," although it has been there for maybe nine maybe nineteen million years. Only very recently has it been known, and even more recently developed so that any of us can go down and enjoy it. It was discovered in 1927 when two ranch boys, chasing a rabbit, saw it disappear into a hole. Investigation led them to discover a human skeleton thirty feet down there in an opening four feet wide. Further exploration revealed an incredibly beautiful and extensive cavern which probably is even grander than Carlsbad Caverns in New Mexico. Today the place has a reception center, smooth trails, electric lights, guides, an elevator inside, and a 4,000-foot all-weather air strip outside, and people are streaming through.

Let me not try to gush about it here, lest I take away some of the element of expectancy and surprise.

But go! Go expecting to find Aladdin's treasure and Aladdin himself; be prepared for rooms that could hold a baseball field including the bleachers; study even the ageless dripstone and flowstone "players," the colossal choristers in their cathedral of incredibly glorious color and form, and endless other exciting "shows."

The location: signs on U.S. 66, just 22 miles west of Seligman, Arizona, announce its presence, one mile south of the highway over a paved road, altitude 5,600 feet — delightful.

Its name? Grand Canyon Caverns. Because they are colorful like the Canyon, and contemporary in age, and second in tourist appeal only to the Grand Canyon itself.

192

# XVII.   SUN STROKE!

The world is well aware that the region between Houston and San Francisco has by gosh the best of everything and knows it. Our Arizona children memorize details of regional superiority long before they learn the catechism or the facts of life. And our performance is seasonal, fluctuating with the intensity of our sunshine; in winter we point with pride to our achievements, but in summer we brag of our worst as well as our best. "Nobody goes to church in my state," the governor of Arizona said one August. "Our summers are so hot we have no fear of hell."

We are both competitive and cooperative in our bragging, which has become so important that it affects our literature, our oratory, our art, our music, and surely our popularity. A few of us — oafish showoffs — become obnoxious with it, but outsiders quickly sense that these have lost caste even at home. The rest of us are perhaps the most altogether welcome missionaries the world has ever known.

Some of our gems are hoary but hallowed; for instance, that concerning the Arizonan to whom St. Peter at the Pearly Gates said, "Well come on in, but you won't like it." We love these favorites best of all and, perhaps surprisingly, so do our listeners. We use them and any new quips with equal ardor. We vie at creation, but we are not above appropriating apt bits that originate in the heathen hinterlands of Manhattan, Canada, or Florida. We ask only the privilege of laughing with you after each narration, and of being loved for the laughing.

And so — with that sedate prologue, I can now report officially that a sea serpent 200 feet long was observed crossing the Arizona desert in the heat of last July.

He had a large dorsal fin, small front legs with webbed toes, and a benign countenance. Scientists trailing him said that he crawled out of the Colorado River when blocked by Glen Canyon Dam, turned eastward to the Rio Grande, thence swam on down to the Gulf of Mexico. Apparently the thing minded its own business — which is significant — and left the world none the worse for its appearance.

You are not to scoff, for you too may stay here to experience the effects of our heat. Psychiatrists and psychologists suggest that because physical enervation follows too much sinning, we suffer more from frustrations and failures, and so for inner compensation we dream up supernatural phenomena. The more down-to-earth Joe simply says, "It's the heat." No matter. At least such tales are the symptoms of summer, and the better ones have taken prominent place in our Arizona folklore. Flying saucers, for instance — remember them? Just let the desert heat soar above 100 degrees, and lo, little men pop out of the sky in all manner of craft. They of course are *green* little men, green being a color for coolness. Thus we reflect our wishful thinking.

One August day the eminent Dr. F. Bruce Russell, described as a retired psychoanalyst, reported the discovery of an Arizona civilization 80,000 years old, built by a race of men nine to twelve feet tall. Mummified remains of the men, also of the dinosaurs they had tamed as beasts of burden, had positively been found. Via the Associated Press and other news agencies, the report created quite a flurry for a few sizzling days, but nothing came of it. September arrived and the prehistoric giants were forgotten before the Phoenix (and San Francisco) Giants' sudden upsurge of baseball power,

194

moving into their league championship. People decided that Dr. Russell must indeed have suffered from the heat. But next August a party of surveyors came onto man tracks three times the size of ordinary men's tracks, and followed them for miles before losing them. They were not far from Dr. Russell's cave of the giants. "Can we hope," asked our scholarly university scientists, "that a few of the giants survive?" Well, can we?

Ah me. We can *hope* for anything; we can even hope that this confounded summer heat will let up on some distant glorious day. They say it always has, but as of this sweltering moment I doubt it. Thus our mental state is revealed.

It is revealed more impressively when we fellow sufferers gather for mutual refrigeration and sympathy, especially if we have been able to capture a transient dude from distant places and force him to listen. Truly we ply him with fantastic facts. And truly he is wise if he acts duly credulous and impressed, for then we will buy him endless cooling concoctions, we will label him a brother in the Lodge, we will proclaim him a Man Among Men. But if he grins sneeringly, or especially if he tries to top our tempestuous tales of temperature — the hell with him.

For the permanent record I now append a few of our representative proclamations, thrown loosely into their respective categories, starting with

## The Climate

Climate hypnotizes all southwesterners into believing that being sinless is hardly worth while; we just don't think there could *be* any better living conditions Up There.

\* \* \*

An Arizonan drove back east to see his ninety-year-old mother who was about to die of sinus trouble, arthritis, asthma, hay fever, cancer, and tuberculosis. He rushed his spare tire into the bedroom and opened the valve. The air thus released was so wonderful that she got well and lived thirty-seven more years.

\* \* \*

Theme song of sun-country health seekers: "I came here thirty years ago to die, and look at me now!"

\* \* \*

Admiral Byrd's men were in an igloo at the South Pole in February, huddled close around the one little oil stove they had. All were shivering, except one overgrown boy from Arizona. Presently even he felt the chill, and said, "Gosh, I bet it shore is cold tonight in Flagstaff."

\* \* \*

It got so cold so suddenly one night in northern Arizona that the flame in a farmer's lantern froze solid and he broke it off and tossed it aside. His dog barked, and the bark froze solid right there in the air. Then the farmer lay down to sleep, and he froze solid.

When spring came, the farmer began to stir again, but the thaw caused the flame to ignite the dried prairie grass and was about to burn the man up. The same thaw also thawed out the dog's bark, and it woke the farmer and enabled him to escape unharmed.

\* \* \*

A loyal citizen of Arizona died back east and they put him in the big oven to cremate his body. After two hours of it they peeked in. The man sat up comfortably and shouted, "SHUT THAT DOOR! I come from Arizona and can't stand a cold draught!"

\* \* \*

A boy from the irrigated desert area around Phoenix went to Houston, Texas, to attend college. The very first week he wrote back: "Dear Mom and Pop: You know that stuff which flows

196

through the canals onto our farm lands in Arizona? Well, it falls right out of the sky over here."

\* \* \*

During the war an Arizona boy who had never been off his native desert was suddenly transferred to Milwaukee, where he encountered his first snow. He was dancing with excitement when a northerner spoke.

"Ain't you never seen snow before?"

"Nope," said the Arizonan, "but I've seen rain once."

\* \* \*

It never gets very hot in Arizona; anybody who says it does is a damned Californian. Mercury in Arizona frequently reaches the top of the thermometer, but that's because it swells with pride for being in Arizona.

\* \* \*

A soldier, long stationed at Yuma, Arizona, died and went to hades — and promptly sent back to Yuma for his blankets.

\* \* \*

"Gosh, does the wind always blow this way?" a newcomer asked a native up in Tuba City, Arizona.

"No sir, only half the time," the native replied. "Other half, she blows the other way."

\* \* \*

One sandstorm got so thick in Tucson that a prairie dog was found digging ten feet above ground. It's so dry out there that neither fish, ducks, nor frogs have ever learned to swim. When a rancher says, "Well, I see the river's up," he means there's a sandstorm blowing.

\* \* \*

197

A citizen of Phoenix died and of course (as Tucson folk would say) went down below. The devil soon was showing him around the place. They entered this chamber and that, seeing how imps stoked the fire and generally kept things hellish. The ex-Phoenician kept mopping his brow. Finally he spoke up.

"Gosh, it certainly is hot down here."

"Yes, yes it is," Satan nodded. "But it's not humid. It's a healthful, dry heat."

"Phooey!" scoffed the man from sun-baked Phoenix. "I've heard that old guff before!"

"Oh sure you have," Satan smiled affably. "Fact is, you told it. That's why you're here."

\* \* \*

In Arizona's sunshine you can't judge a woman by her clothes. Insufficient evidence.

\* \* \*

In southern Arizona the burros, deer, antelope, and cattle are all hairless, the afternoon blows having sandpapered them slick.

\* \* \*

Hot in Arizona? It ain't the heat, it's the whewmidity.

\* \* \*

A few drops of rain fell on a native of southern Arizona and he fainted. Had to throw four buckets of sand on him to bring him to.

\* \* \*

Tucson's "warm" winters? Listen, bud, every February weekend there it gets so cold the fires all freeze. Mexicans grind them up and sell them for chili peppers.

\* \* \*

Gets so dry at Gila Bend, Arizona, the postmaster has to staple stamps to letters. So dry in Scottsdale they have to prime the mourners at funerals.

\* \* \*

The devil himself carries a palm leaf fan in Arizona.

\* \* \*

At midday in Arizona the lizards hang by their tails on the shady side of cactus to keep their bellies from frying.

\* \* \*

My dog's nose got so hot last August he burnt a hole in the back screen door.

\* \* \*

Two easterners in blue serge suits started across the Arizona desert in July. When their car stopped at a filling station, the suits got out and went to the rest room. The men had melted out of them.

\* \* \*

It never rains. Only reason an Arizona home needs a roof is to have a place to put the TV aerial.

\* \* \*

God gave Arizona sand for a beach, but forgot the ocean.

\* \* \*

It never rains. Oh, it did rain once in Arizona. An eight-inch rain — the drops were eight inches apart. Even if it rained now it would be an hour before we could see it; mud, from the dust in our air, would have to fall that long before we could look for clear water. Rain is such a stranger in Arizona that our State Highway

199

Department has put up signs to tell the water which way to flow when, if and as it ever falls.

\* \* \*

A cloud heading from San Diego to Phoenix was almost exhausted, but on the SP railroad at Yuma it found an open water tank, got a transfusion and made it on in.

\* \* \*

A storm came to Arizona, but the raindrops dried before hitting the ground; only their hulls fell. Two men, lost on the desert, squeezed ten bushels of the hulls and extracted a short gallon of water, thus saving their lives.

\* \* \*

Water stays so low in Arizona streams that all the minnows have sunburned backs.

\* \* \*

A cold wave hit our desert; so cold that fourteen inches of ice formed on Roosevelt Lake. Dry ice, of course.

\* \* \*

High wind? Ha! An Arizona kite is an iron shutter with a log chain for a tail.

\* \* \*

Get's so cold in northern Arizona the woodpeckers drum on flint rocks to create sparks they can step on and keep their feet warm.

\* \* \*

A cowboy tried to outrun a sudden Arizona norther. When he finally raced into the home corral, his horse's front quarters were in a sweaty lather and its hind quarters were frozen stiff.

\* \* \*

## SUN STROKE!

An asthma sufferer went to Prescott on August 30 and was completely cured in 30 minutes. But when winter struck on September 30, he took pneumonia and died in 30 minutes.

\* \* \*

A letter addressed to Dehydrated, U.S.A., was delivered to Tucson.

\* \* \*

A one-time Phoenix car dealer named Clark Smith wrote this commentary, which he titled "Summer Complaint":

> Pen me a poem, write me a song,
> Tell me why summer lasts so long.
>
> Early to bed, and early to rise,
> If it ain't mosquitoes, then it's flies!
>
> Straight from the devil, you can't deny
> Is a cold in the head in the month of July.
>
> If there's anything duller than pickled potato,
> It's another platter of sliced tomato!
>
> A pox on people who sun to look
> Like the antique hide of a leather book.
>
> I hope the suns of guns all fry
> Who say it ain't hot because the air is dry.
>
> Loafing's fine in bright, short britches,
> But the green, green grass — alas it itches!
>
> Pen me a poem, write me a song,
> Tell me why summer lasts so long!

201

## The People

Twenty million of the nearly 200 million Americans visit Arizona every year. The remaining 180 million wish they could.

\* \* \*

What's our favorite crack about Arizona? The Grand Canyon.

\* \* \*

A cattleman and an engineer went together to see the Grand Canyon for the first time. The vastness of it overwhelmed them. The cowman said, "Hell of a place to lose a cow." The engineer said, "I'd like to have a dollar a yard to fill it."

\* \* \*

One Arizona ranch boy never left the home range until he was twenty, so loyal to horses and cattle was he. Then he went to town for the first time, and came back married. Pop was pleased, and helped his son build a home seven miles up the canyon. But one day the son came out alone. "Well, Son," Pop asked, "how's your wife doin'?"

"I come out to get another'n," he replied. "That'n stepped in a gopher hole and broke her leg last night, so naturally I had to shoot her."

\* \* \*

Further evidence that we are freedom-loving individualists is seen in the account of two Arizona Indians who came in to a white preacher to be married.

"Do you love this woman?" the preacher asked the man.

"No, ugh," the brave replied.

"Well, do you love this man?" he addressed the woman.

"Ugh, no."

"You don't love each other?" The preacher was distressed.

202

"Then why do you want to get married?"
The lady Indian answered for both: "Him got blanket, me got blanket. Too damn cold sleep alone."

\* \* \*

Arizona has more Democrats than a cactus has thorns. All Arizona Republicans ultimately go to heaven; the Democrats don't have to, they have something better here.

\* \* \*

An Arizona motorist died suddenly and went Up. But he just sat quietly in his golden chair and stared off at the heavenly landscape floating by on clouds. Finally a voice behind him asked, "Mighty pretty, isn't it?"
"Sure is. Cain't beat scenery like that."
"Well then, why don't you fly out amongst it and take part in things Up Here?"
The man turned around and in some embarrassment recognized Saint Peter. "Oh, pardon me, Sir. I didn't realize I was out of Arizona yet."

\* \* \*

No Arizonan has ever been known to tell a lie. But one farmer of the region has lately come under some suspicion; when he wants to feed his hogs, he has to get another man to call 'em.

\* \* \*

An Arizonan is a person with too much heat, too much dust, too much tan, and too much crust.

\* \* \*

Arizona ranch women are hardy. One of them found ten sticks of dynamite left by a blasting crew. Mistaking them for wood, she put the dynamite sticks in her kitchen stove. Next day her husband was telling about it in town.

"Yes sir, gents, it blowed my house clean acrost th' canyon, tore down th' main windmill, ripped up two miles of bobwire fence, and killed forty steers in th' south pasture. And let me tell you I got a mighty sick wife on my hands, too."

\* \* \*

"What denomination do you belong to?" a boy was asked in an eastern Bible school.

He replied, "Arizona."

## The Products

Arizona has more cows and less milk, more mines and less metal, more rivers and less water, more sun and less shade, than any other place in the universe.

\* \* \*

All of the finest motion pictures are written about Texas, financed in California, but filmed in Arizona.

\* \* \*

Finest food in the world is enjoyed by the citizens of Arizona. It is not the vapid stuff of the North and East, but is rich, fragrant, tangy, spicy. A Detroit Marine sergeant was sent down here. He ordered a bowl of chili. Pepper in it was no thicker than usual, but he took one bite, threw the bowl against the wall and shouted, "Blaze, you son-of-a-gun, blaze!"

\* \* \*

Wild life is important in Arizona. Many new species of animals develop here. Most recent discovery is the hibehin. It has short

204

front legs and very long rear ones. Females lay eggs at the top of a hill. As these roll down, friction heat causes them to hatch. The young ones then start upward and spend all their lives climbing. The older they get the higher they live, for they can go in only the one direction. They are very ferocious; only way to escape them is to run downhill.

\* \* \*

Rattlesnakes? Many species are found throughout North America, but Arizona has only one kind — the worst. "One of them bit a hoe handle I had," says Hassayampa Jones, "and the handle swelled up big as a fireplace log. That night I put it on the fire in my cabin, where me and my dogs and my burro slept. Wind drove some smoke into the room. It was so poison it killed my dogs and my burro, drove the pack rats out of the attic, tarnished the walls, and finally killed me. Even the buzzards all died when they tried to pick my bones."

\* \* \*

No state can equal Arizona in the extraordinary quality of its birds. Following are just a few of the species that resort guests have identified through the bottom of a martini glass: Emerald Throated Dowager. Ruffled Spouse. Double Breasted Seersucker. Great American Regret. Red-Eyed Vertigo. Morning Grouse. Midnight Bed Thrasher. Extra-Marital Lark.

\* \* \*

Although we don't like to admit it, Arizona has a few criminals. But they live a hard life here. Consider the mental state of this poor outlaw, after just one effort at honest thievery:

Seems that a Rochester, N. Y., couple moved west (according to old friend and columnist Don Dedera, in Phoenix), taking the wife's ailing mother with them. Somewhere on the Arizona desert they stopped for rest and refreshments, and while there, the mother

205

suddenly died. The man covered his mother-in-law's body with blankets and a tarp, then tied it on the car-top luggage rack for transportation into town. Dutifully he drove to the police station, and with his wife went inside to report the death.

While they were inside, our poor thief stole their car!

## *The Tourists*

In the final reckoning, newcomers and tourists to Arizona have made this state magnificent. Number One analysis of them probably is the following epic poem written by Herbert A. Leggett and first published in the *Arizona Progress* monthly, issued by the Valley National Bank. Herb's contributions to Arizona humor and folklore have been distinguished, so with his permission I now reproduce his memorable

### SONG OF HIGHER-WATER

In the land of Heebie-Jeebie,
By the restless Big-Sea-Water,
Lies the village called Manhattan —
With its teeming marts and smokestacks,
With its murky, man-made canyons,
With its tribes of paleface hunters
Madly stalking Heap-Much Wampum.

There, for long, dwelt Higher-Water
With his squaw and two papooses,
Mid the raucous shouts of hucksters,
Mid the wailing of the foghorns,
Mid the din of trucks and taxies,
Lost among the milling millions —
Till no longer could they bear it.

206

## SUN STROKE!

So it was, one wintry morning,
When the frost was on the windshield
And the angry gales were snarling,
Higher-Water's soul was troubled
As he crouched before the campfire,
Sore beset with aching sinews
And the pangs of mental chilblains.

"Woe is us," he sadly muttered
As he dragged his torpid carcass
To the cellar of the wigwam,
Where ancestral Spirits rested;
Where celestial Spirits hovered;
Where intrepid Spirits bubbled;
To commune with them, he thirsted.

After many visitations,
Interspersed with strong libations,
Higher-Water sprang to action,
Calling forth to Pokey-Haunt-Us,
Who was shoveling out the driveway,
"By the Sun-God in the heavens,
Let us get the Hades from here."

Pokey-Haunt-Us shrieked, ecstatic,
Jumped with joy the pale papooses,
At the prospect of a journey,
At the wonderful decision,
At the valor of their father,
Fortified with potent Spirits
And the hope of new horizons.

So they journeyed, south and westward,
With their Lares and Penates,

207

Swift and eager, like keen hunters,
Over plains and mountain ranges,
Over muddy swollen rivers,
Over swamps and craggy gorges,
Till they came to Arizona.

"This is it," they cried, enraptured
As the sunland stretched before them,
Captivated by the desert,
By the richly tinted landscape,
By the flora and the fauna,
By the warmth of sun and people
In the tranquil Open Spaces.

So they pitched their tent, and tarried,
Never more to roam or wander,
Aping all the native customs,
Joining in the local pow-wows,
While the young ones grew to maidens,
Wedded now to winged warriors
In the Sky Force of the nation.

Here you'll find them, if you care to
Where the Indian Summer lingers
From October until April,
Singing songs of golden sunsets,
Singing songs of silver starlight,
Singing songs like this to beckon
Those not yet in Arizona.

# APPENDICES

# FOR FURTHER READING

The major libraries of the state offer 50 or more fact books
(and hundreds of fiction) containing information about Arizona.
Many are now out of print (that is, not available through book
stores or from the publishers) and many are too old or limited in
scope except for persons doing specialized research. But the following recommended list will be found excellent for most modern
students or other readers who may want further knowledge of this
region.

*Arizona The Wonderland*, George Wharton James. 1917.
Though long out of date, this is still a favorite.

*Arizona; A History Of The Youngest State*, James H.
McClintock.
This history ends in 1915, but is the best available up
to then.

*History Of Arizona*, Edward H. Peplow. 1958.

*Under Turquoise Skies*, William H. Robinson, 1928.
Another early classic.

*Arizona, The History Of A Frontier State*, Rufus K. Wyllys.
1950.

*Men And Women Of Arizona*, Rufus K. Wyllys. 1940.

*Arizona Pageant*, Madeline F. Paré and Bert Fireman.

*March Of Arizona History*, Anne M. Peck.

*Arizona For Boys And Girls*, Dorothy Robinson.

Of special interest in relation to Arizona Indian symbols:
*A Study Of Navaho Symbolism*, by Newcomb, Fishler and
Mary C. Wheelwright.
Published in 1956 by The Peabody Museum, Cambridge,
Mass.

*Book Of The Hopi,* by Frank Waters.
Published in 1963 by Viking Press.

*Indian Silversmithing* by W. Ben Hunt.
Published in 1960 by Bruce Publishing Co., Milwaukee, Wis.

*The New Trail.* An Indian school yearbook for 1941.
Available in the Phoenix Public Library, Arizona Room.

# INDEX

213

216

218

219

# ABOUT THE AUTHOR

OREN ARNOLD has published almost 50 books, several of which have been related to Arizona, and more are in preparation. One was a first-prize-winning Literary Award Novel; all have won wide acclaim for enjoyable reading and depth. In addition, he has published more than 2,000 articles in America's major magazines, and his works appear in countless anthologies.

He is a native Texan who with his bride "discovered" Arizona on their honeymoon, and stayed. They have three daughters, all honor graduates of Arizona schools. Mr. Arnold lives and works in a highly picturesque Indian pueblo-type home of sun-cured adobe bricks, in Phoenix.

During his career he has been awarded the governor's plaque "for distinguished service to Arizona," also the Golden Key proclaiming him "Outstanding Man of The Year" in Phoenix. Many other honors have come to him, both for his professional work and civic services. *Writer's Digest* has called him "the dean of western-American authors."

\* \* \*

THE FRONTISPIECE, an exquisite study of Indian "still life," is a reproduction of a life-sized painting by the distinguished scholar and authority on American Indian culture, Mr. EARL G. HAMMOCK of Phoenix. No other artist has even approached his sensitivity in arrangement nor his perfection of minute detail in depicting the beautiful creations of the red folk of the Southwest. Each of the items in this painting represents the finest in Indian artistry: a delicately woven Navaho rug or "blanket," a Navaho necklace of turquoise, a Hopi basket, a San Ildefonso "pot" fired in gleaming ebony, and a Hopi Kachina doll. The decorative corn is grown by several tribes.

The painting now hangs in the home of the author.